Contents

An Analysis of the Navy's Fiscal Year 2015 Shipbuilding Plan

Summary

The Department of Defense (DoD) submitted the Navy's 2015 shipbuilding plan, which covers fiscal years 2015 to 2044, to the Congress in July 2014.[1] The total costs of carrying out the 2015 plan—an average of about $21 billion in 2014 dollars per year over the next 30 years—would be one-third higher than the funding amounts that the Navy has received in recent decades, the Congressional Budget Office (CBO) estimates. The Navy's 2015 shipbuilding plan is very similar, but not identical, to its 2014 plan with respect to the Navy's total inventory goal for battle force ships, the number and types of ships the Navy would purchase, and the proposed funding to implement the plans.

The Navy Plans to Buy 264 Ships Over the Next 30 Years

The Navy's 2015 shipbuilding plan states that the service's overall inventory goal (in military parlance, its requirement) is 306 battle force ships. The Navy's shipbuilding plan falls short of meeting the service's inventory goals for some types of ships in some years, although generally the shortfalls are smaller than in previous years' plans.

Under the 2015 plan, the Navy would buy a total of 264 ships over the 2015–2044 period: 218 combat ships and 46 combat logistics and support ships (see the top panel of Table 1). Given the rate at which the Navy plans to retire ships from the fleet, that construction plan would not achieve a fleet equal to the inventory goal of 306 ships until 2019 under new rules for counting ships that the Navy implemented this year or until 2022 under the old counting rules.

CBO Estimates the New-Ship Construction Costs in the Navy's Plan At About $19 Billion per Year

The Navy estimates that buying the new ships specified in the 2015 plan would cost $500 billion over 30 years, or an average of $16.7 billion per year—slightly less than the costs of the 2014 plan (see the bottom panel of Table 1). (Unless otherwise indicated, all dollar amounts in this report reflect budget authority in 2014 dollars.) Those figures apply solely to the construction of new ships—the only type of costs reported in the Navy's 30-year shipbuilding plan. Other activities typically funded from the Navy's budget accounts for ship construction—such as refueling nuclear-powered aircraft carriers and outfitting new ships with various small pieces of equipment after the ships have been built and delivered—would, in CBO's estimation, add $1.9 billion to the Navy's average annual shipbuilding costs under the 2015 plan. (Between 2009 and 2014, the cost of those other activities averaged $1.9 billion per year.) Including those extra costs would increase the average annual cost of the Navy's 2015 plan to $18.6 billion, slightly less than the cost of the 2014 plan.

Using its own models and assumptions, CBO estimates that the cost of new-ship construction in the Navy's 2015 plan will total $566 billion over 30 years, or an average of $18.9 billion per year. Including the costs of refueling aircraft carriers and other items, such as outfitting new ships, raises the overall average cost of the Navy's plan to $20.7 billion per year, CBO estimates. That figure is slightly less than CBO's estimate of the average annual cost of the Navy's 2014 plan.

CBO's estimate of the cost of new-ship construction in the Navy's 2015 shipbuilding plan is $66 billion, or 13 percent, higher over the next 30 years than the Navy's estimate. CBO's estimate is 6 percent higher than the Navy's for the first 10 years of the plan, 14 percent higher for the following decade, and 20 percent higher for the

---

1. Department of the Navy, *Report to Congress on the Annual Long-Range Plan for Construction of Naval Vessels for FY 2015* (June 2014), http://go.usa.gov/FYZR (PDF, 3.4 MB).

Table 1.

The Navy's 2014 and 2015 Shipbuilding Plans

	2014 Plan (2014–2043)	2015 Plan (2015–2044)	Change From 2014 to 2015
	Number of Ships Purchased Over 30 Years		
Combat Ships			
Aircraft carriers	6	6	0
Ballistic missile submarines	12	12	0
Attack submarines	47	48	1
Destroyers	70	65	-5
Littoral combat ships	66 [a]	66 [a]	0
Amphibious warfare ships	19	21	2
Subtotal	220	218	-2
Combat Logistics and Support Ships	46	46	0
Total	266	264	-2
	Costs of New-Ship Construction[b] (Billions of 2014 dollars)		
Total Cost Over 30 Years			
Navy's estimate	518	500	-18
CBO's estimate	596	566	-30
Average Annual Cost			
Navy's estimate	17.3	16.7	-0.6
CBO's estimate	19.9	18.9	-1.0
Average Cost per Ship			
Navy's estimate	1.9	1.9	0
CBO's estimate	2.2	2.1	-0.1
Memorandum:			
Average Annual Costs of All Activities Typically Funded From Budget Accounts for Ship Construction			
Navy's estimate	19.2	18.6	-0.6
CBO's estimate	21.8	20.7	-1.1

Source: Congressional Budget Office based on data from the Department of the Navy.

a. Under the 2014 and 2015 plans, the Navy will have 52 littoral combat ships in service after 2029. However, because each of those ships is expected to be in service for 25 years, the Navy will begin buying replacements in 2030.

b. Costs of new-ship construction exclude funds for some activities that are typically funded in the Navy's shipbuilding accounts, such as refueling of nuclear-powered aircraft carriers, ship conversions, construction of ships that are not part of the Navy's battle force (oceanographic survey ships, for instance), training ships, outfitting and postdelivery (which include the purchase of many smaller tools and pieces of equipment that are needed to operate a ship but are not necessarily provided by the manufacturing shipyard as part of ship construction), and smaller items. Costs for the mission packages for littoral combat ships, which are not funded in the Navy's shipbuilding accounts, also are not included.

final 10 years (see Figure 1). The difference widens over time in part because the Navy, in its constant-dollar estimates and in contrast with CBO, does not appear to have accounted for the fact that costs of labor and materials have traditionally grown faster in the shipbuilding industry than in the economy as a whole. Also, the Navy

and CBO used different estimating methods and assumptions regarding the designs and capabilities of future ships. CBO's estimate of the total cost of the Navy's plan over the next 30 years, including all ship construction activities, is 11 percent higher than the Navy's estimate.

Figure 1.

Average Annual Costs of New-Ship Construction Under the Navy's 2015 Plan

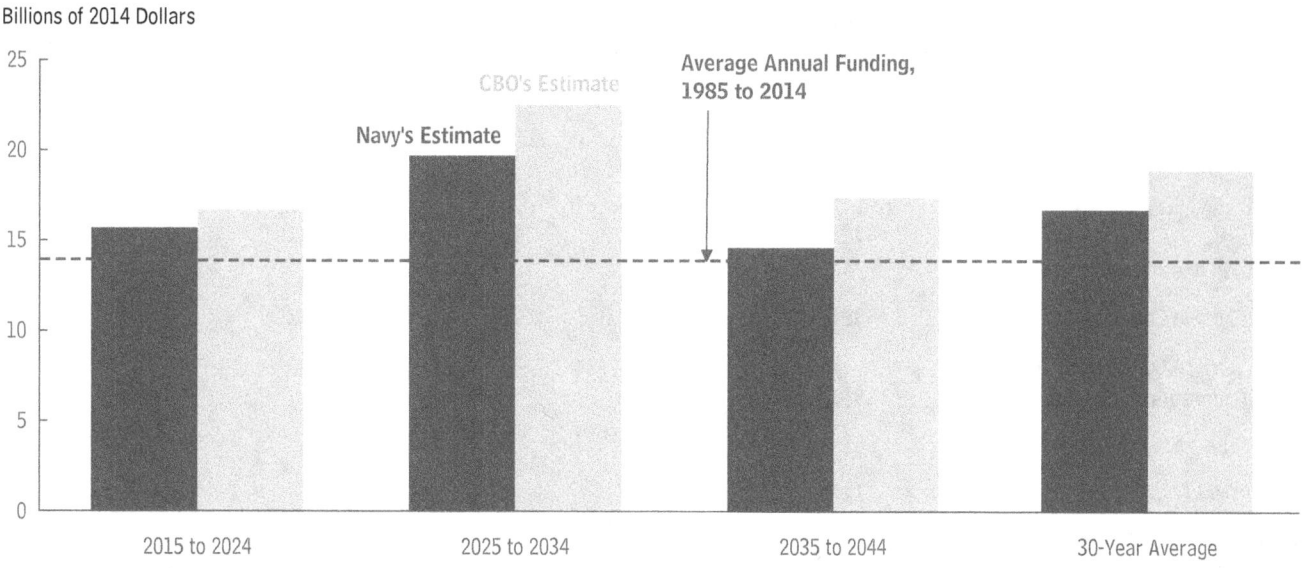

Billions of 2014 Dollars

Source: Congressional Budget Office based on data from the Department of the Navy.

Note: Costs of new-ship construction exclude funds for some activities that are typically funded in the Navy's shipbuilding accounts, such as refueling of nuclear-powered aircraft carriers, ship conversions, construction of ships that are not part of the Navy's battle force (oceanographic survey ships, for instance), training ships, outfitting and postdelivery (which include the purchase of many smaller tools and pieces of equipment that are needed to operate a ship but are not necessarily provided by the manufacturing shipyard as part of ship construction), and smaller items. Costs for the mission packages for littoral combat ships, which are not funded in the Navy's shipbuilding accounts, also are not included.

CBO's Estimate of Costs Over the Next 30 Years Is One-Third Higher Than What the Navy Has Spent Over the Past 30 Years

If the Navy receives the same amount of funding (in constant dollars) for new-ship construction in each of the next 30 years that it has on average over the past three decades, it will not be able to afford its 2015 plan. CBO's estimate of $18.9 billion per year for new-ship construction in the Navy's 2015 shipbuilding plan is 36 percent above the historical average annual funding of $13.9 billion. And CBO's estimate of $20.7 billion per year for the full cost of the plan is 32 percent higher than the $15.7 billion the Navy has spent on average per year for all items in its shipbuilding accounts over the past 30 years.

The Navy Would Probably Need to Purchase Substantially Fewer Ships to Comply With Caps on Defense Funding

The shipbuilding plan, at least for 2015 through 2019, is based on an assumption of funding at the President's requested level—a level that exceeds the amounts

scheduled under current law, which caps discretionary funding through 2021. In submitting its report, the Navy described the plan as "difficult to execute" under current fiscal constraints, and it separately identified changes it would make to the plan if funding for defense equals the amounts scheduled under current law: The Navy would buy 8 fewer ships, including 3 fewer destroyers and 1 fewer attack submarine, between 2015 and 2019; it would charter and lease 3 fleet oilers rather than buy them; and it would put 6 destroyers in a reduced status.[2] However, the identified changes suggest that the Navy would try to cut shipbuilding less than other activities, because if the Navy were to reduce its shipbuilding spending proportionally with the rest of its spending and lower total spending by enough to meet the caps, the service would probably need to cut roughly twice as many ships.

---

2. In a reduced status, the ships would not be operated and would have only caretaker crews. Because they would not be retired, though, they could be restored to full operational status in a year's time.

Table 2.

The Navy's Goals for Its Force Structure

	Goals for a 313-Ship Fleet in the Navy's 2005 Force Structure Assessment	Goals for a 313-Ship Fleet in the Navy's 2010 Force Structure Assessment	Goals for a 306-Ship Fleet in the Navy's 2012 Force Structure Assessment
Aircraft Carriers	11	11	11
Submarines			
Ballistic missile	14	12	12
Attack	48	48	48
Guided missile	4	4	0
Large Surface Combatants	88	94	88
Small Surface Combatants and Mine Countermeasures Ships[a]	55	55	52
Amphibious Warfare Ships	31	33	33
MPF(F) Ships	12	0	0
Combat Logistics Ships	30	30	29
Support Ships			
Joint high-speed vessels	3	10	10
Other[b]	17	16	23
Total	**313**	**313**	**306**

Source: Congressional Budget Office based on data from the Department of the Navy.

Note: MPF(F) = Maritime Prepositioning Force (Future).

a.   Includes littoral combat ships, Oliver Hazard Perry FFG-7 frigates, and Avenger class mine countermeasures ships.

b.   Includes command ships, salvage ships, ocean tugs, ocean surveillance ships, and tenders.

Ship Purchases and Inventories Under the 2015 Plan

The Navy's 2015 shipbuilding plan, submitted to the Congress by the Deputy Secretary of Defense on July 1, 2014, reflects the Navy's goal of 306 battle force ships. That goal, first described by the Navy in a report to the Congress in January 2013, was based on a force structure assessment conducted by the Navy in 2012.[3] It replaced the 313-ship goal developed in the 2005 force structure

---

3.   Department of the Navy, *Report to Congress: Navy Combatant Vessel Force Structure Requirement* (January 2013), http://tinyurl.com/kvhspjs. Battle force ships comprise aircraft carriers, submarines, surface combatants, amphibious warfare ships, and combat logistics and some support ships. For a more extensive discussion of the history of the Navy's force structure goals, see Ronald O'Rourke, *Navy Force Structure and Shipbuilding Plans: Background and Issues for Congress*, Report for Congress RL32665 (Congressional Research Service, August 1, 2014).

assessment and updated in a 2010 force structure assessment (see Table 2).

This report does not evaluate the validity of the goals identified by the Navy, such as the fleet's ability to fulfill its missions in the national military strategy. Rather, the report assesses the costs of the Navy's 2015 shipbuilding plan, the effects of that plan on the force structure, and the extent to which the plan would satisfy the Navy's goals for major components of the U.S. fleet. (For a discussion of the major types of ships in the Navy's fleet and the roles they play, see Box 1.)

Total Ship Purchases and Inventories

The Navy intends to buy 7 ships in 2015 and a total of 44 ships between 2015 and 2019—the period covered by DoD's 2015 Future Years Defense Program, a five-year funding plan that DoD updates annually (see Figures 2 and 3). Thereafter, the Navy would buy an additional 220 ships through 2044, for a total of 264 ships over

Box 1.

The Roles of Major Types of Ships in the Navy's Battle Force Fleet

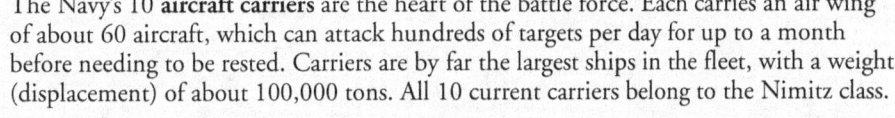

**Nimitz Class
Aircraft Carrier**

The Navy's 10 **aircraft carriers** are the heart of the battle force. Each carries an air wing of about 60 aircraft, which can attack hundreds of targets per day for up to a month before needing to be rested. Carriers are by far the largest ships in the fleet, with a weight (displacement) of about 100,000 tons. All 10 current carriers belong to the Nimitz class.

**Ohio Class Ballistic
Missile Submarine**

Strategic ballistic missile submarines carry one of the major parts of the U.S. nuclear deterrent, up to 24 Trident missiles with one to eight nuclear warheads apiece. The Navy has 14 Ohio class ballistic missile submarines, each of which displaces about 19,000 tons when submerged, in that strategic role. In addition, the Navy has converted 4 submarines of that class to a conventional guided missile (SSGN) configuration. Those SSGNs carry up to 154 Tomahawk missiles as well as special-operations forces.

**Los Angeles Class
Attack Submarine**

Attack submarines are the Navy's premier undersea warfare and antisubmarine weapons. Since the end of the Cold War, however, they have mainly performed covert intelligence-gathering missions. They have also been used to launch Tomahawk missiles at inland targets in the early stages of conflicts. The Navy has 55 attack submarines, 41 of which belong to the Los Angeles class. At 7,000 tons, they are less than half the size of ballistic missile submarines.

**Arleigh Burke Class
Destroyer**

Large surface combatants, which include cruisers and destroyers, are the workhorses of the fleet. They provide ballistic missile defense for the fleet and for regional areas overseas. They defend the Navy's aircraft carriers and amphibious warfare ships against other surface ships, aircraft, and submarines. They also perform many day-to-day missions, such as patrolling sea lanes, providing an overseas presence, and conducting exercises with allies. In addition, they are capable of striking land targets with Tomahawk missiles. Most of the Navy's surface combatants displace about 9,000 to 10,000 tons.

**Freedom Class
Littoral Combat Ship**

Small surface combatants include frigates and littoral combat ships. Frigates today are used to perform many of the same day-to-day missions as large surface combatants. Littoral combat ships are intended to counter mines, small boats, and diesel electric submarines in the world's coastal regions. More routinely, they also patrol sea lanes, provide an overseas presence, and conduct exercises with allies. They range in size from 3,000 to 4,000 tons. The Navy plans to retire all of its remaining frigates in 2015.

**Wasp Class Amphibious
Assault Ship**

**San Antonio Class
Amphibious Transport Dock**

The Navy has six classes of **amphibious warfare ships**. Three classes, referred to as **amphibious assault ships** (also known as large-deck amphibious ships or helicopter carriers), are the second-largest types of ships in the fleet at 40,000 to 45,000 tons. They form the centerpiece of amphibious ready groups, and each can carry about half the troops and equipment of a Marine expeditionary unit. In addition, they can carry as many as 30 helicopters and 6 fixed-wing Harrier jump jets; alternatively, they can carry up to 20 Harriers or short take-off and landing versions of the Joint Strike Fighter. The other three classes are divided into two types: **amphibious transport docks** and **dock landing ships.** Two of those ships together provide the remaining transport capacity for a Marine expeditionary unit in an amphibious ready group. They range in size from 16,000 to 25,000 tons.

**Supply Class Fast Combat
Support Ship**

The many **combat logistics and support ships** in the Navy's fleet provide the means to resupply, repair, salvage, or tow combat ships. The most prominent of those vessels are fast combat support ships, which operate with carrier strike groups to resupply them with fuel, dry cargo (such as food), and ammunition. Logistics and support ships can be as small as 2,000 tons for an oceangoing tug or as large as 50,000 tons for a fully loaded fast combat support ship.

Source: Congressional Budget Office.

Note: Ship silhouettes are not to scale.

Figure 2.

Annual Ship Purchases and Inventories Under the Navy's 2015 Plan

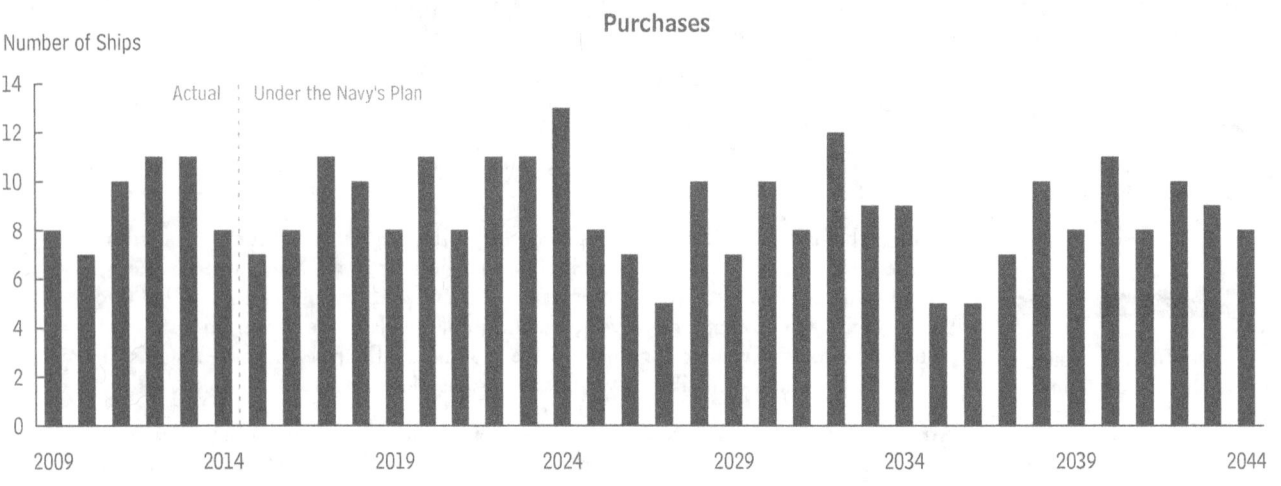

Purchases

Number of Ships

Actual | Under the Navy's Plan

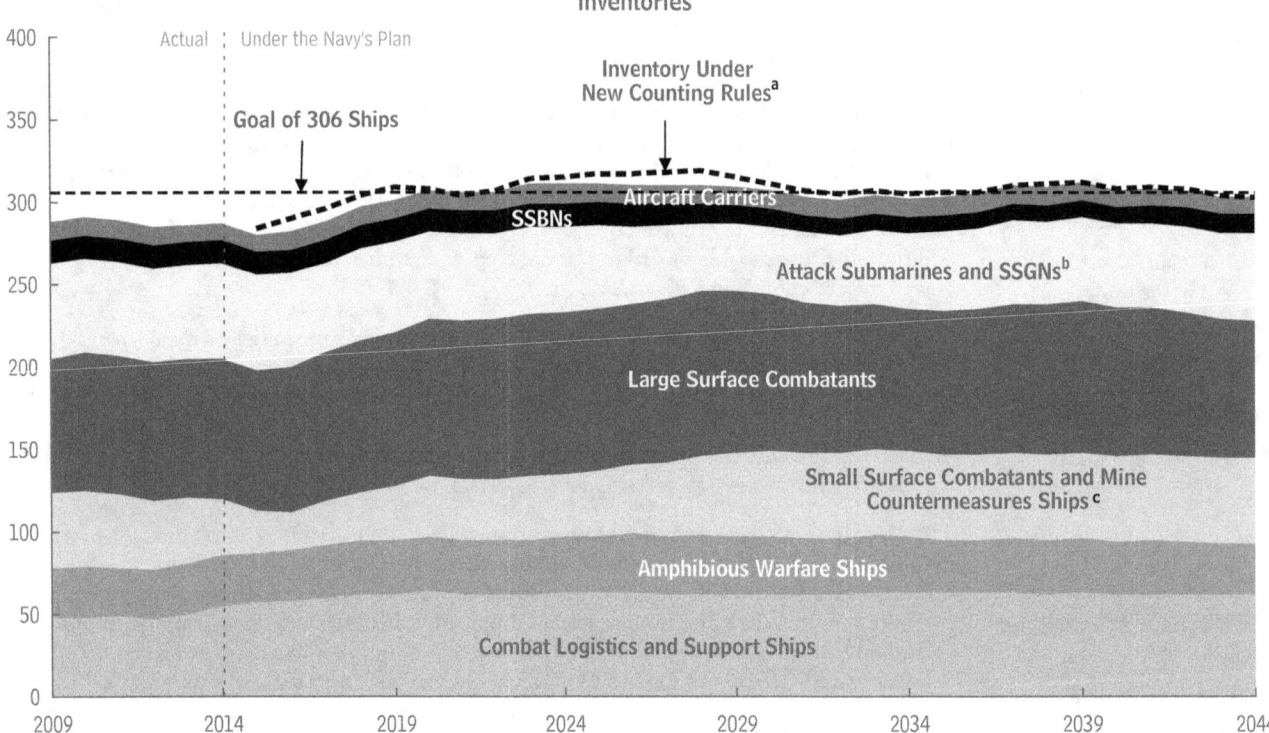

Inventories

Actual | Under the Navy's Plan

Inventory Under
New Counting Rules[a]

Goal of 306 Ships

Aircraft Carriers

SSBNs

Attack Submarines and SSGNs[b]

Large Surface Combatants

Small Surface Combatants and Mine
Countermeasures Ships[c]

Amphibious Warfare Ships

Combat Logistics and Support Ships

Source: Congressional Budget Office based on data from the Department of the Navy.

Notes: The colored parts of the chart reflect the Navy's old counting rules.

SSBNs = ballistic missile submarines; SSGNs = guided missile submarines.

a.   Effective with the 2015 President's budget and shipbuilding plan, the Navy is modifying its method for counting battle force ships. The changes affect a small number of ship classes designated as (very) small combatants or logistics and support ships. Specifically, the Navy will now count Cyclone class patrol combatants that are based overseas (in the theater of operations) but not those that are based in the United States. It will treat Avenger class mine countermeasures ships the same way. The Navy will now also include the 2 hospital ships operated by the Military Sealift Command in the battle force. Patrol combatants and hospital ships did not count under the old rules, whereas all mine countermeasures ships did count, not just those in-theater.

b.   Although the Navy does not plan to build more SSGNs, four will be in service through the mid-2020s.

c.   Small surface combatants and mine countermeasures ships include littoral combat ships, Oliver Hazard Perry FFG-7 frigates, and Avenger class mine countermeasures ships.

Figure 3.

Annual Ship Purchases, by Category, Under the Navy's 2015 Plan

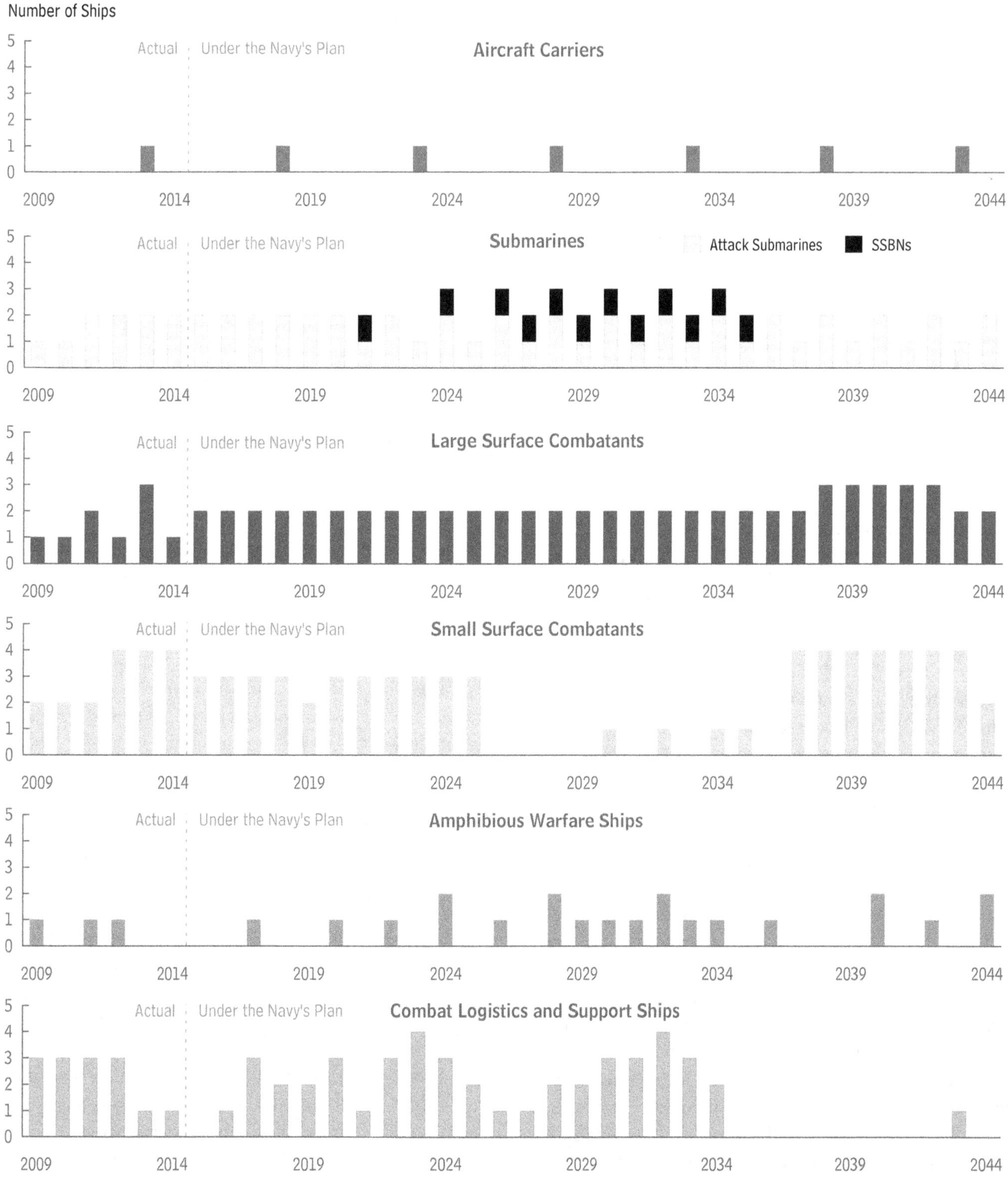
Number of Ships
Actual
Under the Navy's Plan
Aircraft Carriers
Submarines
Attack Submarines
SSBNs
Large Surface Combatants
Small Surface Combatants
Amphibious Warfare Ships
Combat Logistics and Support Ships
0
1
2
3
4
5
2009
2014
2019
2024
2029
2034
2039
2044

Source: Congressional Budget Office based on data from the Department of the Navy.

Note: SSBNs = ballistic missile submarines.

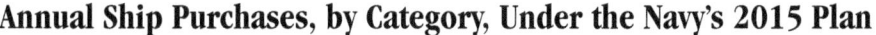

30 years, or an average of about 9 per year. The pace of shipbuilding would be slightly faster, on average, in the near term than later on. The Navy plans to purchase an average of about 10 ships annually between 2015 and 2024, a little less than 9 ships per year between 2025 and 2034, and 8 ships per year between 2035 and 2044.

Effective with the President's 2015 budget and the 2015 shipbuilding plan, the Navy has modified which ships are counted as battle force ships. The changes in the counting rules involve a small number of ship classes designated as (very) small combatants or logistics and support ships. The Navy is now counting as battle force ships Cyclone class patrol combatants that are based overseas (in the theater of operations), although it is not counting those that are based in the United States. It will treat Avenger class mine countermeasures ships the same way. The Navy is also now including in the battle force the 2 hospital ships operated by the Military Sealift Command. Under the old rules, patrol combatants and hospital ships did not count in the battle force, whereas all mine countermeasures (not just those that are in-theater) did count in the battle force. The Navy projects that, at the end of 2015, it will have 284 ships in the fleet under the new counting rules and 274 ships under the old rules. The patrol combatants and the mine countermeasures ships are slated to retire from service in the 2020s, and the 2 hospital ships will retire in 2035. The 2015 shipbuilding plan does not replace those vessels. Thus, by 2036 and beyond, the size of the battle force is planned to be the same under either set of counting rules.

The 2015 plan would not achieve the intended force of 306 ships until 2019 under the Navy's new counting rules or 2022 under the old rules. The Navy would meet its overall goal of 306 ships for 21 years of the 30-year plan under the new counting rules and for 16 years under the old rules. Under the new rules, the shortfall is never more than 1 to 3 ships, except for the 2015–2017 period (see the bottom panel of Figure 2). The Navy achieves its force structure goal much sooner under the 2015 plan than under the 2014 plan, which would not have reached the goal of 306 ships until 2037. The Navy's goal for battle force ships would be realized more quickly under the 2015 plan partly because of the change in counting rules, but largely because the Navy now intends to retain in its inventory 7 cruisers and 2 amphibious ships that it proposed to retire in 2014 under the 2014 plan. The Congress opposed the early retirement of those ships.

All together, the Navy would buy 2 fewer ships over 30 years under the 2015 plan than it would have under the 2014 plan. The composition of ship purchases—particularly the mix of combat ships and logistics and support vessels—is virtually the same under the 2014 and 2015 plans.

Combat Ships

Under the 2015 plan, the Navy envisions buying 218 combat ships—aircraft carriers, submarines, large and small surface combatants, and amphibious warfare ships—between 2015 and 2044. That total is 2 fewer than specified in the 2014 plan for 2014 through 2043. Those purchases would still leave the Navy short of its inventory objectives for ballistic missile and attack submarines for significant parts of the 2015–2044 period (see Figure 4). In contrast, there are essentially no projected shortfalls in large surface combatants or amphibious warfare ships (which represents an improvement from the 2014 plan). For aircraft carriers, the Navy would meet or exceed its goal of 11 ships throughout the 2014–2044 time frame, except for brief periods from 2015 to 2016 and 2040 to 2044. For small surface combatants, the Navy plans to replace its frigates and mine countermeasures ships with littoral combat ships (LCSs); it would not reach its objective of having 52 LCSs in the fleet until 2028, one year earlier than in the 2014 plan. (The Navy has stated that any future plans designed to increase the survivability and lethality of its small surface combatants would not change its inventory goal for those ships.)

Ballistic Missile Submarines. The 2015 shipbuilding plan calls for buying the first replacement for the Ohio class ballistic missile submarines in 2021 and for purchasing 12 such submarines, also known as SSBN(X)s, in total (see Figure 3); those boats would begin to enter the fleet in 2028. (The Navy estimates that the lead submarine will take about seven years to build and that an additional two to three years will be needed to complete testing before it is ready for regular operations.) However, the retirement of Ohio class submarines as they reach the end of their 42-year service life means that the Navy's inventory of ballistic missile submarines (SSBNs) would fall below the stated goal of 12 by 1 or 2 submarines between 2030 and 2041 (see Figure 4). In particular, between 2032 and 2040, the Navy would have 10 SSBNs.

Figure 4.

Annual Inventories Versus Goals for Selected Categories of Ships Under the Navy's 2015 Plan

Number of Ships

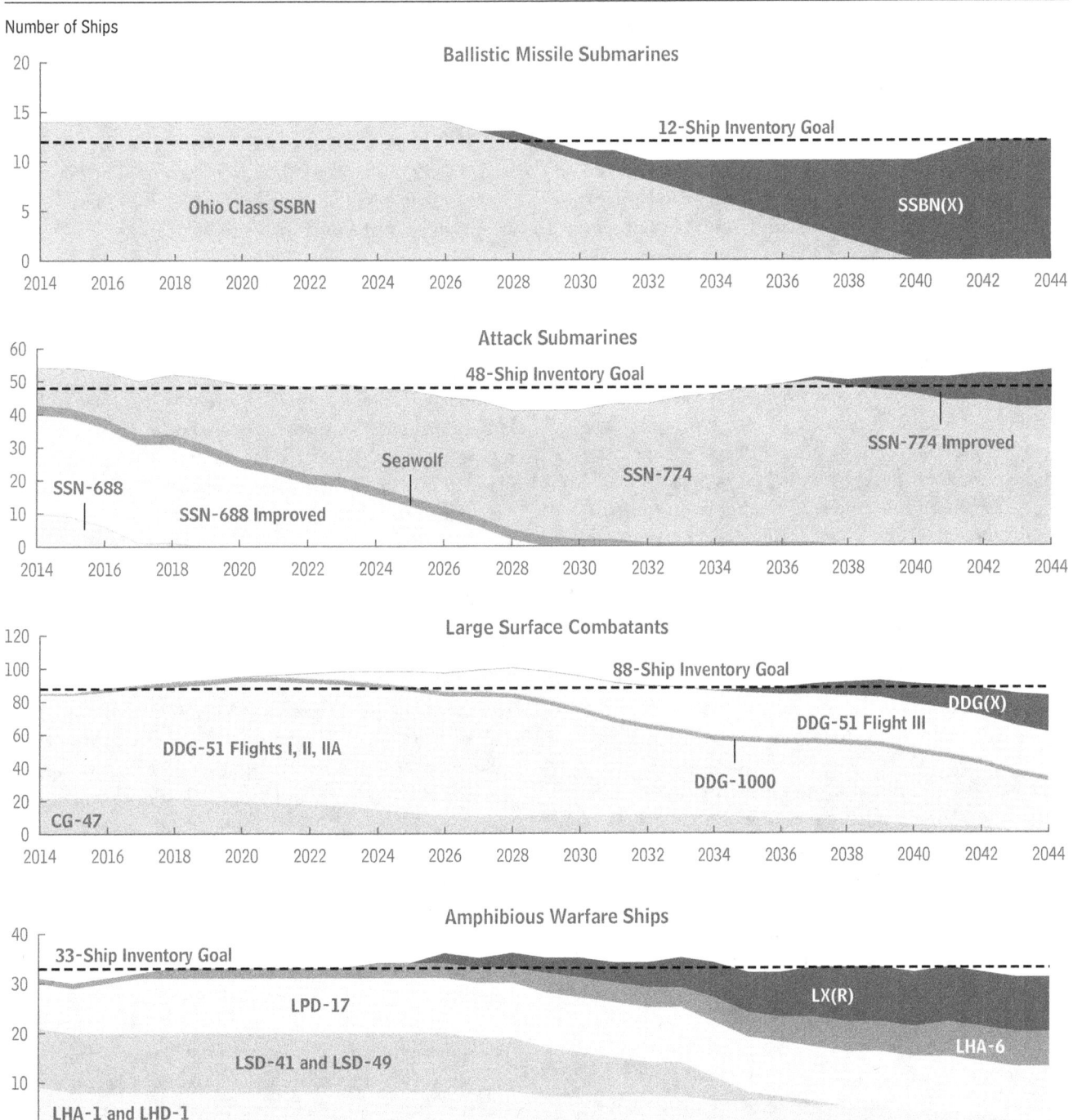

Source:　Congressional Budget Office.

Note:　SSBN = ballistic missile submarine; SSN = attack submarine; DDG = guided missile destroyer; CG = guided missile cruiser; LSD = dock landing ship; LHA and LHD = amphibious assault ship; LPD = amphibious transport dock; LX(R) = amphibious ship replacement.

Attack Submarines. Under the 2015 plan, the Navy would purchase 48 attack submarines (SSNs) through 2044, which would not be enough to keep that force at the stated goal of 48 throughout the next 30 years. The number of attack submarines would decline from 48 in 2024 to a low of 41 in the 2028–2030 period and then would increase to 51 or more after 2039. The decline would result because, in 2014, the Navy began retiring Los Angeles class attack submarines (SSN-688s), which were generally built at rates of 3 or 4 per year during the 1970s and 1980s, as they reached the end of their service life. The Navy would replace those submarines with Virginia class attack submarines (SSN-774s) and their successors at rates of generally 1 or 2 per year.

Large Surface Combatants. The 2015 shipbuilding plan calls for buying 65 destroyers—5 fewer than in the 2014 plan—based on the existing Arleigh Burke class destroyer (DDG-51) design (see Table 1 on page 2). Those purchases, along with the Navy's plan for modernizing its cruiser force (and several amphibious ships), would allow the Navy's inventory of large surface combatants to meet or exceed the goal of 88 ships for most years over the next 30. (For a discussion of the Navy's modernization plan for cruisers and amphibious warfare ships, see Box 2.) Specifically, the number of such ships would meet or exceed the goal in each year through 2033 (with the exception of 2015) and fall short only in the 2034–2035 and 2042–2044 periods.

The Navy's assumptions about the service lives of its large surface combatants remain the same under the 2015 plan as under the 2014 plan. The 2014 plan incorporated an assumption that all 34 Arleigh Burke class destroyers commissioned after 2000 would have a service life of 40 years and that the 28 destroyers of that class commissioned in 2000 and earlier would remain in the fleet for 35 years. Historically, very few cruisers or destroyers have served in the fleet longer than 30 years.[4] If the Navy's large surface combatants serve for 30 years instead of the longer intended lives, and if the Navy's acquisition of such ships matches the pace of the 2015 plan, then the Navy will experience a substantial shortfall of those ships relative to its goal.[5]

---

4. See Congressional Budget Office, *Resource Implications of the Navy's Fiscal Year 2009 Shipbuilding Plan* (June 9, 2008), p. 25, www.cbo.gov/publication/41703.

5. See Congressional Budget Office, *An Analysis of the Navy's Fiscal Year 2014 Shipbuilding Plan* (October 2013), p. 26, www.cbo.gov/publication/44655.

Amphibious Warfare Ships. The current shipbuilding plan calls for buying 21 amphibious warfare ships through 2044—2 more than specified in the 2014 plan—which would increase the amphibious force from 31 ships today to the goal of 33 by 2018. The force would stay at that size or greater through 2044—except for 2035 to 2036, when the force would fall to 32 ships, and 2040, 2042, 2043, and 2044, when the force would have 32, 32, 31, and 31 ships, respectively. The Navy assumes that it will keep its LHD class amphibious assault ships in the fleet for 43 to 45 years.

Combat Logistics and Support Ships

In its 2015 plan, the Navy envisions buying 46 combat logistics and support ships in the next three decades—the same number as in the 2014 plan. Combat logistics ships include T-AKE dry cargo ships, T-AO oilers, and AOE fast combat support ships; they operate with or directly resupply combat ships that are on deployment. Those planned purchases include 17 new oilers (which provide fuel and a few other supplies to ships at sea) at a rate of 1 per year through the 2020s; that program would conclude in 2033. The plan also includes the purchase of 1 replacement T-AKE dry cargo and ammunition ship in 2043.

Support ship purchases in the Navy's plan include 10 joint high-speed vessels (JHSVs), 4 salvage ships, 5 surveillance ships, 2 tenders, 4 fleet tugs, 2 command ships to replace those in the existing fleet that will retire over the next 30 years, and 1 new afloat forward staging base, a variant of the Navy's mobile landing platform ships.[6] H.R. 83, the Consolidated and Further Continuing Appropriations Act, 2015, which cleared the Congress on December 13, 2014, added funding for 1 JHSV. If signed into law, that legislation will increase the Navy's inventory by one, barring other changes; the effects of that change are not reflected in this analysis.

The only significant change from the Navy's 2014 plan in this category is the decision to retire 2 salvage ships and 2 fleet tugs nine years and four years earlier, respectively, than called for in the previous plan. According to the Navy, the decision to retire those ships earlier was made in order to reduce costs. That action would leave the Navy with 2 salvage ships and 2 fleet tugs in its inventory

---

6. The afloat forward staging base is a ship designed to remain on station overseas for long periods of time, providing support to other naval forces, such as special operations units, patrol craft, or minesweepers.

Box 2.

The Navy's Modernization Plan for Cruisers and Amphibious Ships

The Navy's 2015 plan largely meets the service's inventory goals for large surface combatants and amphibious ships, which the 2014 plan did not. The difference arises primarily from a new proposal for modernizing 11 CG-47 Ticonderoga class cruisers and 3 amphibious dock landing ships. Previously, the Navy had proposed retiring 7 cruisers and 2 amphibious ships (largely as a means to save money), but the Congress rejected those proposals and instead provided funding for operating and modernizing the ships in a special account called the Ship Modernization, Operations, and Sustainment Fund (SMOSF).

In the President's 2015 budget submission, the Navy proposes to lay up (to put in a reduced status for maintenance and modernization) 11 cruisers, which is half the force, and 3 amphibious ships. The ships would be minimally manned while in that reduced status and, as the other 11 active cruisers reach the end of their service life, cruisers in lay-up would be modernized and returned to operational status. Using that approach, the Navy would be able to maintain at least 11 operationally active cruisers (1 for each of the Navy's planned 11 carrier strike groups) through 2034, with the last cruiser retiring in 2044. (The Navy's 2015 shipbuilding plan does not include replacements for the Ticonderoga class cruisers, but the midsized surface combatants planned for the 2030s and 2040s could be designed to perform the same missions as the current cruisers.) The 3 amphibious ships would be put in a reduced status sequentially, so that all 3 would be modernized but only 1 would be in lay-up at a time.

All 22 cruisers would be counted toward the Navy's inventory of battle force ships in each year. The Navy's justification for including the 11 cruisers in lay-up in its inventory is that the cruisers could be brought out of reduced operating status and returned to the fleet within a year's time; cruisers and destroyers that are currently undergoing long-term maintenance of a year or more are also counted as part of the battle force.

If the modernization plan is not implemented and the Navy's cruisers and amphibious ships remain in fully operational status, then all of those ships would probably be retired from the fleet by 2028 (which reflects the retirement schedule under the 2014 plan). The result would be to create larger shortfalls relative to the Navy's inventory goals in later years. If the Navy is able to implement its plan for cruisers and amphibious ships, the service estimates that it will save about $8 billion through 2026.

H.R. 83, the Consolidated and Further Continuing Appropriations Act, 2015, which cleared the Congress on December 13, 2014, rejects the Navy's cruiser and amphibious ship modernization plan. Instead, if signed into law, the legislation will give the Navy authority to lay up and modernize 2 cruisers in 2016, using the funds provided in the SMOSF. It stipulates that no more than 6 cruisers may be in lay-up at any given time. It is not clear how that legislation would affect the long-term inventory of large surface combatants. The legislation did not specify the approach the Navy should take for amphibious ships.

---

until 2023 and 2019, respectively, when replacements enter the fleet. The decision to retire those ships early (even though they are not very expensive to operate) and the consequent gaps in the inventory raise the question of whether the Navy needs 4 ships of each type to support fleet operations. The Navy states in the plan that "if mission workload requires additional ships," it would use leased vessels.[7]

Shipbuilding Costs Under the 2015 Plan

According to the Navy's estimates, carrying out its planned purchases of new ships would cost an average of $16.7 billion per year through 2044—3 percent less than the $17.3 billion average under its 2014 plan (in 2014

---

7. Department of the Navy, *Report to Congress on the Annual Long-Range Plan for Construction of Naval Vessels for FY 2015* (June 2014), p. 13, http://go.usa.gov/FYZR (PDF, 3.4 MB).

Figure 5.

Average Annual Costs of New-Ship Construction Under the Navy's 2014 and 2015 Plans

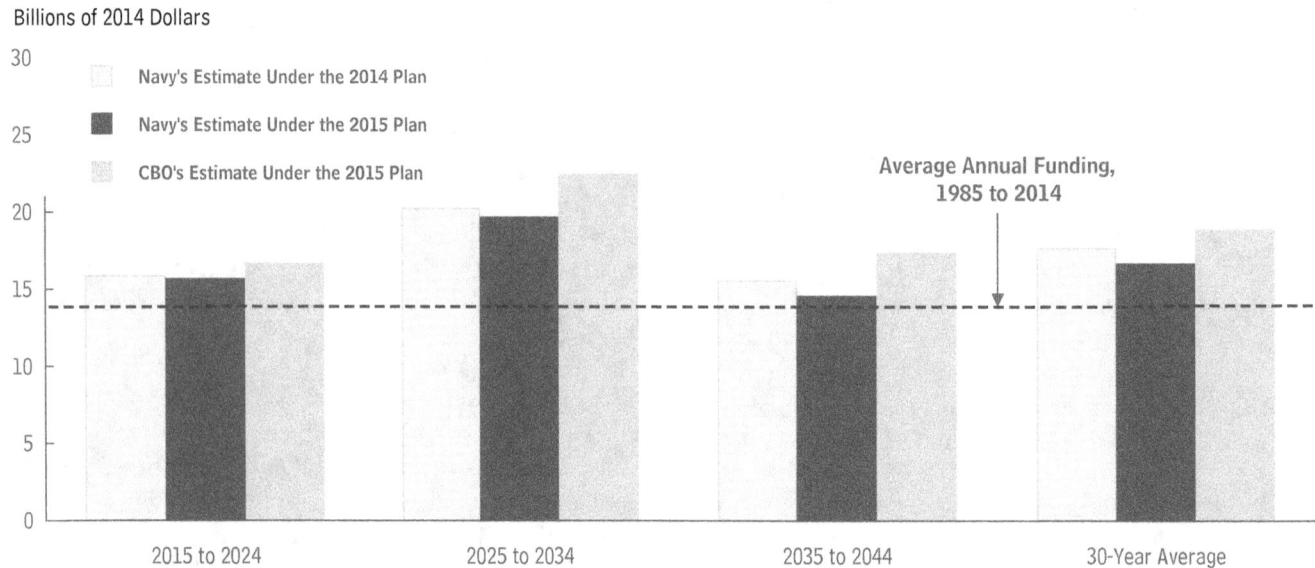

Billions of 2014 Dollars

Navy's Estimate Under the 2014 Plan

Navy's Estimate Under the 2015 Plan

CBO's Estimate Under the 2015 Plan

Average Annual Funding, 1985 to 2014

2015 to 2024   2025 to 2034   2035 to 2044   30-Year Average

Source: Congressional Budget Office based on data from the Department of the Navy.

Note: Costs of new-ship construction exclude funds for some activities that are typically funded in the Navy's shipbuilding accounts, such as refueling of nuclear-powered aircraft carriers, ship conversions, construction of ships that are not part of the Navy's battle force (oceanographic survey ships, for instance), training ships, outfitting and postdelivery (which include the purchase of many smaller tools and pieces of equipment that are needed to operate a ship but are not necessarily provided by the manufacturing shipyard as part of ship construction), and smaller items. Costs for the mission packages for littoral combat ships, which are not funded in the Navy's shipbuilding accounts, also are not included.

dollars). In making its estimates, the Navy divided the time frame of the 2015 plan into three periods: the near term (2015 to 2024), the midterm (2025 to 2034), and the far term (2035 to 2044). CBO also estimated the costs of the Navy's 2015 plan; to price the Navy's ships, it used its own cost models and assumptions, which are explained in detail later in this report. CBO's estimates are $2.2 billion per year, or 13 percent, higher than the Navy's over the next 30 years as a whole, but the differences are smaller for the near term, larger for the midterm, and larger still for the far term (see Figure 5). Including other items that the Navy would need to fund from its budget accounts for ship construction would raise both the Navy's estimates and CBO's estimates by $1.9 billion per year; CBO's estimates of that full cost are 11 percent above the Navy's corresponding figures.[8]

The Navy's Estimates

The Navy's 2015 report offers a frank discussion of the difficulties in estimating the capabilities that the Navy will want ships to have—and thus the cost of those ships—over the three planning periods. For the near

term, the report explains, "The projections in the period are based on our most accurate understanding of required combat capabilities, future defense budget top-lines, and shipbuilding costs based on actual procurements in progress. The cost estimates for this period are the most accurate of the three planning periods." For the midterm, "The accuracy of plan cost estimates diminishes." And for the far term, "Since the strategic environment and state of technology 20–30 years hence are both sure to be much different than they are today, the precision and accuracy of the ship types required and cost projections in this period are much more speculative."[9]

---

8. The Navy has funded shipbuilding through two accounts: Shipbuilding and Conversion, Navy (commonly called the SCN account) and the National Defense Sealift Fund (NDSF), which includes, among other things, funding for the procurement of some types of logistics ships. With the 2015 budget, the Navy proposes disestablishing the NDSF and funding all ships through the SCN account.

9. Department of the Navy, *Report to Congress on the Annual Long-Range Plan for Construction of Naval Vessels for FY 2015* (June 2014), p. 10, http://go.usa.gov/FYZR (PDF, 3.4 MB).

New-Ship Construction Costs. According to this year's plan, in the near term, building new ships will cost an average of $15.7 billion per year (see the top row of Table 3). That number excludes $1.4 billion in cost overruns and sequestration shortfalls for ships that were funded before 2015, which will require additional funds to be paid out in 2015 and 2016. In the midterm, replacing the Navy's current Ohio class ballistic missile submarines drives up the average cost of new-ship construction to $19.7 billion per year. According to the Navy's estimates, building the SSBN(X) will cost $5.5 billion per year in the middle decade of the plan. In the far term, the Navy's estimated costs fall to an average of $14.6 billion annually.

Although the Navy's shipbuilding plan suggests that the midterm will be its most challenging fiscal period, the latter half of the near term (2020 to 2024) will require shipbuilding budgets that are substantially larger than those in the first half of the first decade (2015 to 2019). According to the Navy's estimates, the average budget for new-ship construction rises from $13.7 billion per year for the 2015–2019 period to $17.8 billion per year for the 2020–2024 period (see Figure 6).

Total Shipbuilding Costs. As in previous shipbuilding plans, the Navy's latest estimates exclude other costs that it would have to pay out of its budget accounts for ship construction. Specifically:

■ Costs of refueling nuclear-powered aircraft carriers, whose reactors are replaced midway through the ships' service lives,[10] and

■ Other costs, such as those for ship conversions, construction of ships that are not part of the Navy's battle force (oceanographic survey ships, for instance), training ships, outfitting and postdelivery (which include the purchase of many smaller tools and pieces of equipment that are needed to operate a ship but are not necessarily provided by the shipyard when the ship is built), and smaller items.

Including the costs of refueling carriers, as estimated by CBO, would increase the Navy's estimate for the cost of the 2015 shipbuilding plan by $1 billion per year to an average of $17.7 billion a year through 2044.

Adding the $1.4 billion in cost-to-complete funding that will be spent in 2015 and 2016, along with the costs of the other items described above, would boost the Navy's estimate for the full cost of the 2015 shipbuilding plan to $18.6 billion per year, or $1.9 billion more than the Navy's estimate for new-ship construction alone. That figure is 18 percent higher than the average funding for total shipbuilding the Navy has received in the past three decades—$15.7 billion per year.

CBO's Estimates

In CBO's estimation, the full annual cost of the 2015 shipbuilding plan would average $20.7 billion over the 2015–2044 period—32 percent more than the average annual funding the Navy has received in the past three decades. The estimated costs have a fair amount of yearly variation but trend upward for the first two decades of the plan (see Figure 7 on page 16). Looking at the 30-year period as a whole, CBO estimates that:

■ Costs for new-ship construction alone would average $18.9 billion per year, 13 percent more than the Navy's figure of $16.7 billion (see Table 3);

■ New-ship construction plus refueling of nuclear-powered aircraft carriers would cost an average of $19.9 billion per year, 12 percent more than the Navy's figure of $17.7 billion; and

■ All other items would add annual costs of about $900 million, raising CBO's estimate to an average of $20.7 billion per year through 2044, 11 percent more than the Navy's figure of $18.6 billion.

CBO's estimates of the full cost of the plan are only 4 percent higher than the Navy's for the first 10 years but 18 percent higher for the final 10 years. For the near term, CBO's and the Navy's cost estimates are similar because most of the ships that the Navy plans to buy are already under construction and their costs are reasonably well known. For the midterm and far term, however, CBO and the Navy made different assumptions about the size and capabilities of future ships that led to different cost estimates. Generally, CBO estimates the cost of a future ship on the basis of the relationship between the

---

10. In 2010, the Navy transferred funding for refueling nuclear-powered submarines to other accounts (Other Procurement, Navy; Operation and Maintenance, Navy; and Weapons Procurement, Navy) that are not used to purchase ships. Therefore, CBO did not include the refueling costs for submarines in its estimates of future shipbuilding costs.

Table 3.

Average Annual Shipbuilding Costs Under the Navy's 2015 Plan, by Decade

	Near Term (2015–2024)	Midterm (2025–2034)	Far Term (2035–2044)	Total (2015–2044)
	Navy's Estimates (Billions of 2014 dollars)			
New-Ship Construction	15.7	19.7	14.6	16.7
New-Ship Construction and Refueling of Nuclear-Powered Aircraft Carriers[a]	17.1	20.7	15.2	17.7
New-Ship Construction, Refueling of Nuclear-Powered Aircraft Carriers, and Other Items[b]	18.4	21.4	15.8	18.6
	CBO's Estimates (Billions of 2014 dollars)			
New-Ship Construction	16.7	22.5	17.5	18.9
New-Ship Construction and Refueling of Nuclear-Powered Aircraft Carriers	18.0	23.5	18.1	19.9
New-Ship Construction, Refueling of Nuclear-Powered Aircraft Carriers, and Other Items	19.2	24.2	18.7	20.7
	Percentage Difference Between the Navy's and CBO's Estimates			
New-Ship Construction	6	14	20	13
New-Ship Construction and Refueling of Nuclear-Powered Aircraft Carriers	6	13	19	12
New-Ship Construction, Refueling of Nuclear-Powered Aircraft Carriers, and Other Items	4	13	18	11
Memorandum (Billions of 2014 dollars): CBO's Estimate of the Costs of New-Ship Construction Needed to Meet Nearly All All Inventory Goals in Each Year	19.0	22.6	17.6	19.7
Costs of Mission Packages for Littoral Combat Ships	0.4	0.1	0.3	0.3

Source: Congressional Budget Office based on data from the Department of the Navy.

Note: Other items include ship conversions, construction of ships that are not part of the Navy's battle force (oceanographic survey ships, for instance), training ships, outfitting and postdelivery costs (which include the purchase of many smaller tools and pieces of equipment needed to operate a ship but not necessarily provided by the manufacturing shipyard as part of ship construction), and smaller items. Actual costs for the Navy's shipbuilding accounts over the past 30 years averaged about $16 billion per year for all items.

a.   These numbers represent the Navy's estimate for new-ship construction and CBO's estimate for the refueling of nuclear-powered aircraft carriers.

b.   These numbers represent the Navy's estimates for both new-ship construction and cost-to-complete funding for ships purchased in prior years, and CBO's estimates for the refueling of nuclear-powered aircraft carriers and other items.

weight and cost of analogous ships. The resulting figure is then adjusted for factors such as production efficiencies that occur as more ships of the same type are built at a given shipyard simultaneously and additional efficiencies that occur as more ships are built (and learning takes place) over the duration of a production run. CBO also incorporated into its estimates (which are in constant 2014 dollars) a projection that costs for labor and materials would probably continue to grow faster in the shipbuilding industry than in the economy as a whole, as they have for the past several decades; the Navy's estimates do not reflect such faster growth (see Box 3 on page 18). That difference in estimates is much more pronounced in the last decade of the plan, after 20 or more years of

Figure 6.

The Navy's Estimates of the Costs of New-Ship Construction, 2015 to 2024

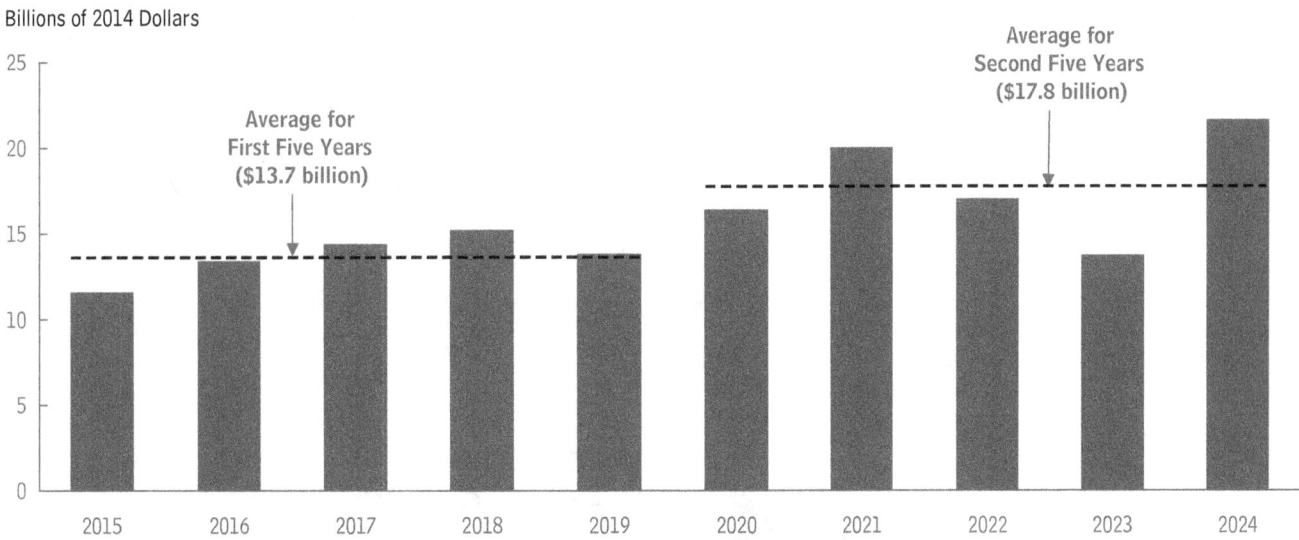

Billions of 2014 Dollars

Source: Congressional Budget Office based on data from the Department of the Navy.

Note: Costs of new-ship construction exclude funds for some activities that are typically funded in the Navy's shipbuilding accounts, such as refueling of nuclear-powered aircraft carriers, ship conversions, construction of ships that are not part of the Navy's battle force (oceanographic survey ships, for instance), training ships, outfitting and postdelivery (which include the purchase of many smaller tools and pieces of equipment that are needed to operate a ship but are not necessarily provided by the manufacturing shipyard as part of ship construction), and smaller items. Costs for the mission packages for littoral combat ships, which are not funded in the Navy's shipbuilding accounts, also are not included.

compounded growth, than in the early years. (For more information on how much of the overall difference between the Navy's estimates and CBO's estimates can be attributed to individual ship programs, see Table A-1 in the appendix.)

Costs of Meeting Nearly All Inventory Goals in Each Year

Under its 2015 shipbuilding plan, the Navy would not build enough ships at the right times to meet the service's inventory goal of 306 battle force ships until 2019 under the Navy's new counting rules and 2022 under the old rules. In particular, the plan would lead to temporary shortfalls relative to the Navy's goals for ballistic missile submarines and attack submarines and, in the far term, for aircraft carriers as well. However, there would be only small and short-lived shortfalls for large surface combatants and amphibious warfare ships (see Figure 4 on page 9).

The Navy does not believe it can prevent the shortfall in ballistic missile submarines. The service life of existing Ohio class submarines cannot be extended because of technical reasons relating to the ships' material condition

(particularly the hull) and reactor life.[11] And building the new class of ballistic missile submarines faster, the Navy argues, would introduce technical risks that would outweigh the risks of having 10—rather than the preferred 12—SSBNs that are deployable for a decade.

Other shortfalls, however, could be avoided or reduced by accelerating or increasing ship purchases relative to those specified in the 2015 shipbuilding plan. To meet most of its existing goals, the Navy could make the following changes to the current shipbuilding plan:

■ To prevent the attack submarine force from falling below the inventory goal of 48 submarines, the Navy could accelerate the purchase of 7 submarines. Specifically, it could purchase 7 additional submarines

---

11. The service life of submarines is determined by many factors; two major ones are the condition of their hulls and the energy remaining in their reactor cores. Submarines can only "cycle"—that is, submerge and surface a limited number of times before they need to be retired. In addition, after a nuclear reactor has produced a certain amount of energy, it needs to be retired. Some nuclear submarines can be refueled if the hull has remaining life, but those submarines with "life of the ship" reactor plants cannot be refueled.

Figure 7.

CBO's Estimates of Annual Shipbuilding Costs Under the Navy's 2015 Plan

Billions of 2014 Dollars

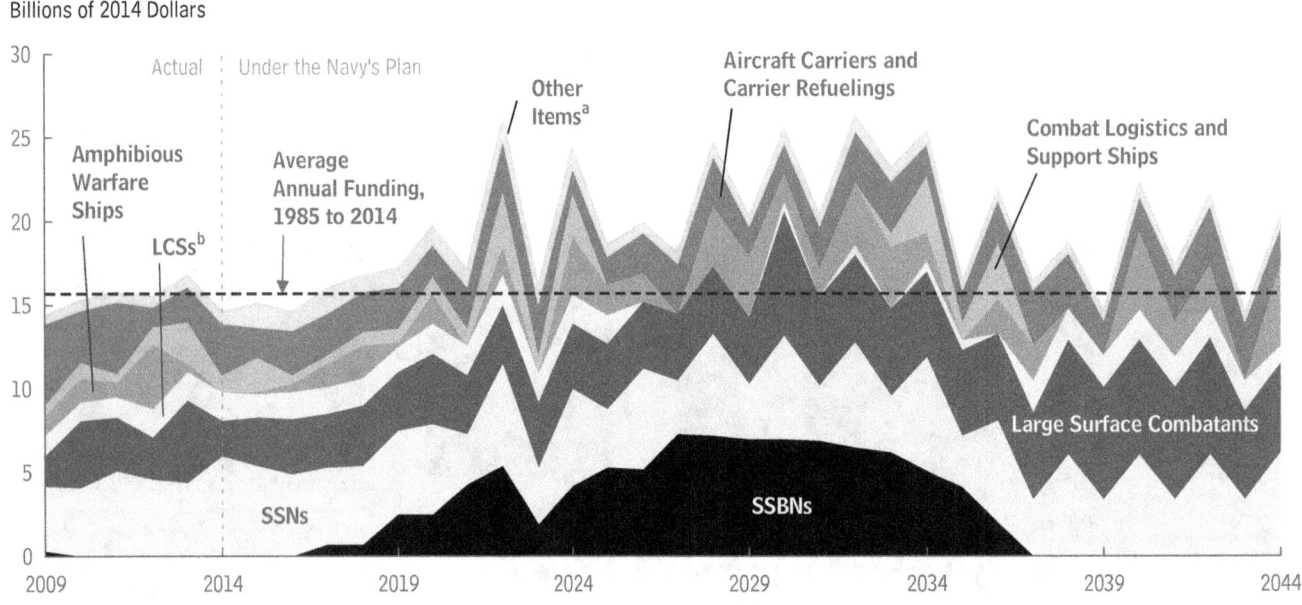

Source: Congressional Budget Office based on data from the Department of the Navy.

Note: LCSs = littoral combat ships; SSNs = attack submarines; SSBNs = ballistic missile submarines.

a.   Other items include funds for ship conversions, construction of ships that are not part of the Navy's battle force (oceanographic survey ships, for instance), training ships, outfitting and postdelivery (which include the purchase of many smaller tools and pieces of equipment needed to operate a ship but not necessarily provided by the manufacturing shipyard as part of ship construction), and smaller items.

b.   Costs for the mission packages for littoral combat ships, which are not funded in the Navy's shipbuilding accounts, are not included.

from 2017 through 2023, increasing the production rate to 3 submarines per year for most of those years. If that increase occurred, the Navy could buy 7 fewer attack submarines between 2025 and 2034 than are called for under the 2015 plan and still maintain the desired inventory.

■ To prevent the carrier force from declining in the 2040s to 10 ships, 1 short of its inventory goal of 11, the Navy could accelerate carrier purchases after 2018 to 1 every four years, rather than 1 every five years.

■ To meet its goal of 88 large surface combatants in the last years of the plan, the Navy could purchase 5 additional destroyers between 2028 and 2037, increasing the production rate to 3 ships per year for five more years. That change would restore the reduction of 5 destroyers that occurred between the 2014 and 2015 plans.

■ To prevent small shortfalls in later years of the plan, the Navy could purchase 2 additional amphibious

warfare ships by 2030. That course of action would allow the Navy to meet its inventory goal of 33 ships in each year after 2017. However, the Navy cannot prevent a shortfall in amphibious warfare ships relative to the Navy's goal in the next few years, because ships of that sort take four to five years to build.

According to CBO's estimates, incorporating the changes described above into the Navy's 2015 plan would raise costs significantly in the first decade of the plan and by very small amounts in the second and third decades. The annual cost of new-ship construction would average $19.0 billion between 2015 and 2024 (instead of $16.7 billion, as in CBO's estimate of the Navy's plan), $22.6 billion between 2025 and 2034 (instead of $22.5 billion), and $17.6 billion between 2035 and 2044 (instead of $17.5 billion). Over the entire 30-year period, new-ship construction would average $19.7 billion per year, compared with $18.9 billion per year for the Navy's plan.

Other approaches to prevent falling short of the Navy's inventory goals could have different costs. For example, if the Navy was able to extend the service life of some existing ships, it would need fewer new ships, thus reducing procurement costs but possibly increasing operation and maintenance costs because older ships tend to be more expensive to operate than newer ships of the same class. Such an approach would not be effective in preventing a shortfall of all types of ships, however. In particular, the Navy's plan already reflects an assumption that most destroyers will be in service for 40 years, although historically very few have served longer than 30 years. Consequently, CBO does not expect that those ships could serve for an even longer period to prevent the shortfall in large surface combatants. By contrast, extending service life for amphibious warfare ships seems more plausible because those ships are already serving for 40 years and the Navy is planning to keep some beyond 40 years. Thus, the Navy could prevent the minor shortfalls in amphibious warfare ships after 2035 by not retiring existing ships and extending their service life by a few years in several cases.

Shipbuilding Given Historical Average Funding

CBO's estimate of $20.7 billion per year for the full cost of the Navy's 2015 shipbuilding plan is 32 percent higher than the $15.7 billion the Navy has spent on average per year for all items in its shipbuilding accounts over the past 30 years. If the Navy's future funding for shipbuilding is in line with its past funding, the Navy will need to reduce substantially its new-ship purchases relative to the number called for in its 2015 plan.[12]

To illustrate how much smaller the fleet of battle force ships would be under that scenario, CBO constructed an alternative shipbuilding plan to meet two criteria. First, the purchase of specific types of ships would be reduced relative to the 2015 plan in rough proportion, with the exception of ballistic missile submarines. The Navy's most senior officials have described replacing the current

Ohio class submarines as the service's top priority; CBO assumed, therefore, that the Navy would purchase all 12 submarines included in its 2015 plan. With the nearly proportional reduction in purchases of other types of ships, the distribution of the fleet in 2044 among types of ships would be about the same as that specified in the 2015 plan, although the number of ships of each type would be smaller. Second, spending would be fairly similar (in inflation-adjusted dollars) during the near-term, midterm, and far-term periods. That alternative plan is not a recommendation by CBO but simply an illustration of the possible consequences of continuing funding for shipbuilding at its historical average amount rather than increasing it, as would be required under the Navy's 2015 plan.[13]

Purchases under that alternative plan would number 195 ships (versus 264 in the Navy's plan) and would consist of the following:

■ 4 aircraft carriers (compared with 6 in the Navy's plan),

■ 12 ballistic missile submarines (there also are 12 in the Navy's plan),

■ 31 attack submarines (compared with 48 in the Navy's plan),

■ 45 destroyers (compared with 65 in the Navy's plan),

■ 47 littoral combat ships (compared with 66 in the Navy's plan),

■ 15 amphibious ships (compared with 21 in the Navy's plan), and

■ 41 combat logistics and support ships (compared with 46 in the Navy's plan).

Under that alternative plan, the battle force fleet in 2023 would be about the same size as in the Navy's plan but by 2044 would number 242 ships, as opposed to the

---

12. For a broader discussion of historical cost trends in Navy shipbuilding, see the testimony of Eric J. Labs, Senior Analyst for Naval Forces and Weapons, Congressional Budget Office, before the Subcommittee on Seapower and Expeditionary Forces of the House Committee on Armed Services, *The Long-Term Outlook for the U.S. Navy's Fleet* (January 20, 2010), www.cbo.gov/ publication/41886.

13. In its report accompanying the 2014 National Defense Authorization Act, the House Committee on Armed Services directed the Navy to provide to the Congress a similar illustration of a shipbuilding plan (starting in 2015) that conforms to historical funding levels. The Navy has not yet responded to that Congressional directive.

Box 3.
Inflation in Shipbuilding

The costs of building future ships depend on the sizes and capabilities of those ships, as well as on the evolution of the cost of building a ship of any given size and capability. The differences between the Navy's and the Congressional Budget Office's (CBO's) estimates of the cost of the Navy's shipbuilding plans arise in part because of differences in the projected future cost of building a ship of any given size and capability.

The Navy provided CBO with an index of shipbuilding costs between 1960 and 2013, which measures the historical growth in the costs of labor and materials used in shipbuilding. To project the increase in those costs for 2014 through 2020, the service extrapolated from that historical experience and also incorporated information from advance pricing agreements, vendor surveys, and projections of the cost of materials from the Bureau of Labor Statistics. For those years, the Navy projects that the index of shipbuilding costs will increase at an average annual rate of 2.9 percent. By comparison, CBO projects that the gross domestic product (GDP) price index, which measures the prices of all final goods and services produced in the economy, will increase at an average annual rate of 1.9 percent during those years. Thus, CBO estimates that the cost of building a given ship (as projected by the Navy's index) will increase between 2014 and 2020 at a rate that is 1.0 percentage point faster per year, on average, than inflation for the economy as a whole. That difference in projected inflation rates is larger than the 0.9 percentage-point difference that CBO found in

its analysis of the Navy's 2014 plan. Since 1984, the difference between the rate of increase in the Navy's shipbuilding cost index and the GDP price index has averaged about 1.3 percentage points per year (see the figure).

The Navy incorporated that projected increase of 2.9 percent per year in shipbuilding costs into its budget request for 2015 and into the associated Future Years Defense Program; both of those documents express costs in nominal dollars. In projecting the constant-dollar costs for its 2015 shipbuilding plan, the Navy converted those nominal dollars to inflation-adjusted dollars using the shipbuilding price index rather than the GDP price index. That is, the 2015 shipbuilding plan incorporates the view that a ship that costs $2.5 billion to build in 2014 will cost the same (in 2014 dollars) to build in 2035.

In contrast, CBO converted the costs of ships from nominal dollars to inflation-adjusted dollars using the GDP price index, thereby reflecting the expectation that inflation in shipbuilding will exceed overall inflation. As noted, cost growth in the shipbuilding industry has exceeded general inflation for most of the past three decades, and CBO lacks an analytic basis for determining when and to what extent the difference between the two growth rates might narrow. Therefore, CBO projects that shipbuilding inflation will outpace inflation as measured by the GDP price index by 1.0 percentage point per year between 2014 and 2020 and by 1.3 percentage points per year—the 30-year historical average—thereafter.

Continued

303 ships in the Navy's plan. The inventory in 2044 would consist of the following ships:

- 8 aircraft carriers (compared with 10 in the Navy's plan),

- 12 ballistic missile submarines (there also are 12 in the Navy's plan),

- 41 attack submarines (compared with 52 in the Navy's plan),

- 69 destroyers (compared with 83 in the Navy's plan),

- 33 littoral combat ships (compared with 52 in the Navy's plan),

- 27 amphibious ships (compared with 31 in the Navy's plan), and

- 52 combat logistics and support ships (compared with 63 in the Navy's plan).[14]

---

14. The alternative plan would also fund one fewer carrier refueling.

Box 3.   **Continued**

Inflation in Shipbuilding

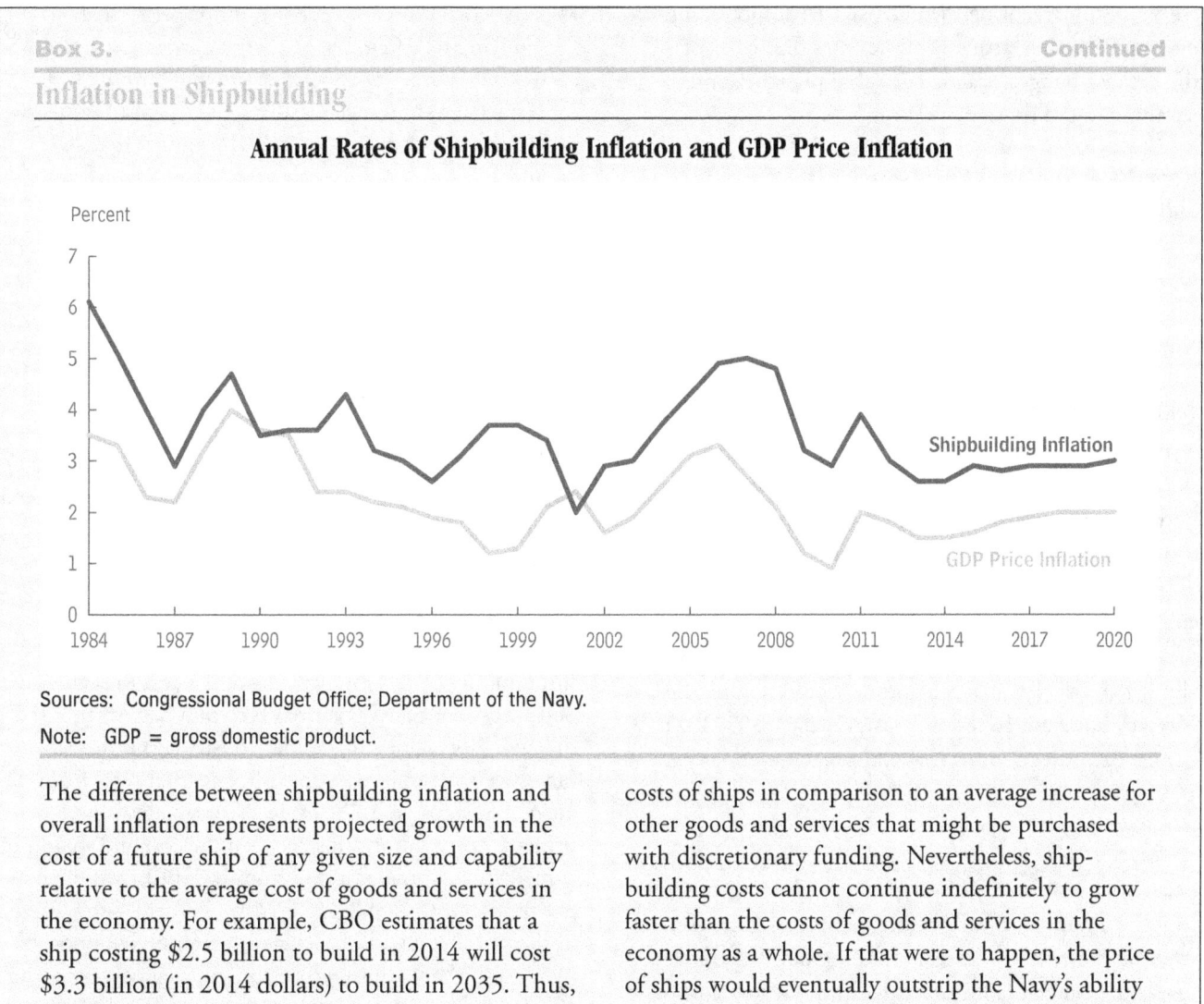

Annual Rates of Shipbuilding Inflation and GDP Price Inflation

Sources: Congressional Budget Office; Department of the Navy.

Note: GDP = gross domestic product.

The difference between shipbuilding inflation and overall inflation represents projected growth in the cost of a future ship of any given size and capability relative to the average cost of goods and services in the economy. For example, CBO estimates that a ship costing $2.5 billion to build in 2014 will cost $3.3 billion (in 2014 dollars) to build in 2035. Thus, CBO's constant-dollar estimates reflect the increased costs of ships in comparison to an average increase for other goods and services that might be purchased with discretionary funding. Nevertheless, shipbuilding costs cannot continue indefinitely to grow faster than the costs of goods and services in the economy as a whole. If that were to happen, the price of ships would eventually outstrip the Navy's ability to pay for even a very small number of them.

Other approaches to staying within historical funding would have different results. If the Navy reduced the number of larger and more expensive ships more sharply than in the alternative plan described above, then the overall fleet would be larger. Conversely, if the Navy preserved the programs of more expensive ships, then the overall fleet would be smaller. Ultimately, decisions about which ships to build would depend on the priorities that policymakers established for certain naval missions relative to others.

Shipbuilding Under the Budget Control Act of 2011

Given the caps on defense funding from 2015 to 2021 that stem from the Budget Control Act of 2011 as amended by the American Taxpayer Relief Act of 2012 and the Bipartisan Budget Agreement of 2013, DoD will receive funding for its base budget—which excludes the cost of overseas contingency operations, such as the war in Afghanistan—that is substantially lower after adjusting for inflation than the funding it received in 2010, when such funding reached its peak. Specifically, after adjusting for inflation, DoD's base budget fell in 2014 to about the same amount that the department received in 2007, and it will remain essentially flat through 2021.[15] Consequently, under current law, DoD faces a choice

15. For a more thorough discussion of the Budget Control Act and its effect on the Department of Defense, see Congressional Budget Office, *Approaches for Scaling Back the Defense Department's Budget Plans* (March 2013), www.cbo.gov/publication/43997.

between implementing the Navy's 2015 shipbuilding plan and exerting strong pressures on other parts of the defense budget, scaling back that plan, or some combination of those two actions.

If the Navy receives the same percentage of DoD's budget during the coming decade and devotes the same percentage of its budget to ship construction that it has historically, the shipbuilding budget would be a little less than $13 billion per year from 2015 through 2021. In comparison, the Navy's 2015 shipbuilding plan would require spending a little more than $17 billion on all shipbuilding activities over the same period, CBO estimates. (During the past 15 years, the Department of the Navy has received about 30 percent of DoD's base budget and has devoted about 10 percent of its funding to shipbuilding.) That amount would be $5.5 billion per year—or 30 percent—below CBO's estimate of the amount required to execute the Navy's 2015 shipbuilding plan. If all shipbuilding programs were cut proportionally, a reduction of that magnitude would require the Navy to purchase 16 fewer ships over the 2015–2021 period than the 63 ships it would purchase under its 2015 plan.

So far, the Navy has not canceled any ship purchases because of insufficient funding, although it has proposed to retire a number of ships early because of fiscal constraints. However, the cuts in funding in 2013 triggered under the Budget Control Act led the Navy to slow or otherwise alter elements of its shipbuilding programs. Funding in 2014 and 2015 would largely, if not completely, make up for the funding lost in 2013.

In an April 2014 report, DoD identified the changes it would make to the Navy's shipbuilding plan and ship operations, along with the resulting inventory, if the current caps on defense funding are left in place.[16] Specifically, the Navy would:

■ Buy 8 fewer ships between 2015 and 2021, including 3 fewer destroyers and 1 fewer attack submarine;

■ Charter and lease 3 fleet oilers rather than buy them;

■ Not refuel the U.S.S. *George Washington*, thereby reducing its inventory of aircraft carriers by 1 and disestablishing its associated air wing (although the Navy later announced that it would plan to refuel the aircraft carrier as part of its 2016 budget request);[17] and

■ Put 6 destroyers in a reduced status (in addition to the cruisers and amphibious ships that the Navy intends to put in a reduced status under its own plans).[18]

Those identified changes suggest that the Navy would try to cut shipbuilding less than its other activities, because if the Navy reduced its shipbuilding spending proportionally with the rest of its spending and cut total spending by enough to meet the caps, the service would probably need to cut roughly twice as many ships.

Outlook for Specific Ship Programs

To estimate the costs of implementing the Navy's 2015 shipbuilding plan, CBO calculated the cost of each of the 264 ships that the Navy intends to purchase from 2015 through 2044. For ships under construction, the estimates were based in part on data for actual costs from the Navy. For ships yet to be built, the estimates were based primarily on relationships between the cost and weight of similar ships in the past. Specifically, CBO used the cost per thousand tons of lightship displacement—the weight of the ship itself without its crew, materiel, weapons, or fuel. CBO then adjusted its estimates to incorporate the effects of "rate" (the reduction in average overhead costs that occurs when a shipyard builds more than one of the same type of ship at a time) and "learning" (the efficiencies that shipyards gain as they produce additional units of a given type of ship). The effects of rate and learning were applied to the estimated cost of the first ship of a class (the lead ship) to determine the estimated costs for all subsequent ships of that class. Thus, CBO's estimate of the cost of the lead ship in a class drove its estimate of the costs of subsequent ships of that class. To estimate the

---

16. Department of Defense, *Estimated Impacts of Sequestration-Level Funding: United States Department of Defense Fiscal Year 2015 Budget Request* (April 2014), pp. 3-3, 4-7 to 4-9, http://go.usa.gov/sZkJ (PDF, 2.2 MB).

17. Sam Langrone, "Stackley: Navy Plans to Refuel Carrier *George Washington*," *USNI News* (July 10, 2014), http://tinyurl.com/mwoodta.

18. To lower costs, the President's 2015 budget proposed putting in a reduced status ("laying up") 11 cruisers and 1 amphibious ship. (The Navy actually proposed laying up 3 amphibious ships, but it would do so sequentially, so there would be only 1 amphibious ship in a reduced status at any point in time.) The budget also proposed modernizing those ships to extend their service life.

costs of ships for which the Navy has yet to develop even notional designs, CBO had to make assumptions about the size and capabilities of those ships. All costs of individual ships described in this section exclude outfitting and postdelivery costs, which typically add about 3 percent to the cost of a ship.

Aircraft Carriers

The 2015 shipbuilding plan states that the Navy's goal is to have 11 aircraft carriers. The Navy intends to buy 6 CVN-78 Gerald R. Ford class aircraft carriers over the 2015–2044 period. Building 1 carrier every five years (referred to as five-year centers) would enable the Navy to have a force of at least 11 carriers almost continuously through 2044, with two exceptions. One exception would be from 2015 to 2016, when the number of carriers would be 10. That temporary decline occurs because the *Enterprise* (CVN-65) was retired in early 2013 after 52 years of service, and the next new carrier, the *Gerald R. Ford* (CVN-78), will not be commissioned until 2016. Any delays in completing that new carrier would extend the period during which the Navy has only 10 carriers. The other exception would be from 2040 to 2044 and beyond. If carriers continued to be built every five years and to serve for 50 years, the Navy's carrier force would fall to 10 in 2040 and remain at that level.[19]

The Navy currently projects that the total cost of the lead ship of the CVN-78 class will be $12.9 billion in nominal dollars over the period from 2001 to 2016, an amount equal to the Congressional cost cap.[20] Using the Navy's inflation index for naval shipbuilding, CBO converted that figure to $14.3 billion in 2014 dollars.[21] That amount is 23 percent more than the amount requested in the President's budget when the ship was first authorized in 2008. The Navy's estimate does not include $4.7 billion in research and development costs that apply to the entire class.

CBO estimates that the total cost of the lead ship of the CVN-78 class will be $13.5 billion in nominal dollars and $14.8 billion in 2014 dollars. To generate that

estimate, CBO used the actual costs of the previous carrier—the CVN-77—and adjusted them for the higher costs of government-furnished equipment in the newer configuration and for more than $3 billion in costs for nonrecurring engineering and detail design (the plans, drawings, and other one-time items associated with the first ship of a new class). Subsequent ships of the CVN-78 class will not require as much funding for one-time items, although they will incur the same costs for government-furnished equipment. All together, CBO estimates the average cost of the 6 carriers in the 2015 plan at $12.8 billion, compared with the Navy's estimate of $12.5 billion (see Table 4).

The final cost of the CVN-78 could be higher or lower than CBO's estimate. Possible reasons for a higher cost include the following:

- The costs of many lead ships built in the past 20 years have increased by more than 30 percent from the original budgeted estimates. CBO's estimate of the cost of the CVN-78 incorporates an amount of growth that falls within the range of historical cost growth for lead ships, and the costs reported for the roughly 80 percent of construction completed to date are consistent with that estimate—but costs have tended to rise more in the latter stages of ship construction, when systems are being installed and integrated. For example, the test program for the carrier could reveal one or more major and possibly expensive problems.

- The Navy has stated that there is a 50 percent probability that the cost of the CVN-78 will exceed its estimate. Specifically, in its most recent selected acquisition report, the Navy stated that it has budgeted an amount for the CVN-78 that covers up to the 50th percentile of possible cost outcomes.

---

19. In addition, if the Navy ultimately does not refuel the U.S.S. *George Washington*, the carrier force would fall to 9 through early 2016 and then remain at 10 until 2023.

20. In its 2015 budget request, the Navy asked for an extra $787 million in nominal dollars in 2015 and 2016 to cover cost growth and additional tooling and vendor services, most of which was anticipated in the 2014 budget request. That amount is included in the Navy's estimate of the total cost to complete the ship.

21. Using a different method, the Navy estimated that the $12.9 billion cost in nominal dollars for the lead ship would equate to just over $15 billion in 2014 dollars. The Navy's calculation is based on a unique method that is not comparable to CBO's method for estimating costs in constant dollars and is not used by the Navy to estimate costs in constant dollars for any other shipbuilding program. If CBO used the Navy's unique method to convert its own estimate for the carrier program (which involves using different carrier-specific inflation indexes for different cost components of the ship) from nominal dollars to constant dollars, CBO's estimate for the cost of the CVN-78 would still be about $600 million more than the Navy's.

Table 4.

Comparison of the Navy's and CBO's Estimates for the Construction of Major New Ships Under the Navy's 2015 Plan

Billions of 2014 Dollars

	Number of Ships Purchased Under the 2015 Plan	Total Costs per Class Over the 2015–2044 Period		Average Costs per Ship Over the 2015–2044 Period		Memorandum: Average Costs per Ship Under the 2014 Plan	
		Navy's Estimates	CBO's Estimates	Navy's Estimates	CBO's Estimates	Navy's Estimates	CBO's Estimates
CVN-78 Gerald R. Ford Class Aircraft Carriers	6	74 [a]	76 [a]	12.5 [a]	12.8 [a]	12.5	12.9
Ohio Replacement Ballistic Missile Submarines	12	79	92	6.6	7.7	6.6	7.4
Virginia Class Attack Submarines	31	88	90	2.8	2.9	2.8	2.8
Improved Virginia Class Attack Submarines (Replacements for Virginia class)	17	49	54	2.9	3.2	3.3	3.2
DDG-51 Arleigh Burke Class Destroyers							
Flight IIA	3	4	4	1.4	1.4	1.6	1.6
Flight III	27	44	51	1.6	1.9	1.8	2.0
DDG(X) Destroyers (Replacements for Arleigh Burke class)	35	63	88	1.8	2.5	2.0	3.4
Littoral Combat Ships							
Flight 0	12	b	6	b	0.5	0.5	0.5
Flight 1	20	b	12	b	0.6	n.a.	n.a.
Total	32	15	18	0.5 [c]	n.a.		
LCS(X)s (Replacements for littoral combat ships)	34	16	16	0.5 [c]	0.5	0.4	0.6
LX(R)s (Replacements for amphibious dock landing ships)	11	16	19	1.4	1.8	1.4	1.8
LHA-6 Amphibious Assault Ships	7	24 [d]	26 [d]	3.7 [d]	4.0 [d]	3.7	4.5
LPD-17 Replacements	3	7	8	2.2	2.6	e	e
T-AO(X) Oilers	17	8	8	0.5	0.5	0.5	0.5

Source: Congressional Budget Office based on data from the Department of the Navy.

Notes: The costs in this table exclude funding for research and development for these ships.

     Relative to Table 1, this table excludes 29 support ships of various types.

     n.a. = not applicable.

a. In CBO's and the Navy's estimates for aircraft carriers, total costs per class include remaining funds for the CVN-78 and CVN-79, but exclude that part of the funding for the carrier the Navy plans to purchase in 2043 that would be budgeted after 2044. CBO's and the Navy's estimates of the average cost per ship exclude the remaining funding for the CVN-78 and CVN-79 but include all of the funding for the carrier slated for purchase in 2043.

b. The Navy did not make a distinction between the existing design for littoral combat ships (LCSs) and an improved LCS design that may be required as a result of the proposal for building a small combatant that is more capable of surviving attacks and more lethal to adversaries. CBO's estimates include some additional funding, roughly estimated, for improving 20 of the LCSs in those ways.

c. The Navy's estimate for the LCSs is $464 million per ship, and its estimate for the LCS(X)—the replacement ship—is $473 million. Those costs exclude the cost of LCS mission packages, which CBO also excluded from its estimates.

d. In CBO's and the Navy's estimates for amphibious assault ships, total costs per class exclude half the funding for the ship that would be purchased in 2044 because that money would be budgeted for 2045. CBO's and the Navy's estimates of the average cost per ship include all of the funding for the ship scheduled for purchase in 2044.

e. CBO did not report these data in its analysis of the Navy's 2014 plan.

Possible reasons for a lower cost than CBO's estimate include the following:

- The Navy and the builder of the CVN-78 recognize that cost growth for lead ships is a significant concern, and they are actively managing the CVN-78 program to restrain costs.

- All of the materials for the CVN-78 have been purchased, and much of the equipment for the vessel is being purchased under fixed-price contracts; those factors essentially eliminate the risk of further cost growth for about half of the projected cost of the carrier.

- The test program might reveal only minor problems. In that case, the cost of the ship would probably be less than CBO's estimate, although it might still exceed the Navy's estimate.

The next carrier following the CVN-78 will be the CVN-79, the *John F. Kennedy*. Funding for that ship began in 2007, the Congress officially authorized its construction in 2013, and appropriations for it are expected to be complete by 2018. The Navy estimates that the ship will cost $11.5 billion in nominal dollars ($160 million more than the estimate under the President's 2014 budget) and $10.6 billion in 2014 dollars. In its selected acquisition report on the CVN-79, the Navy describes its cost estimate as an "aggressive but achievable target." In contrast, CBO estimates that the cost of the ship will be $12.6 billion in nominal dollars and $11.5 billion in 2014 dollars, about 8 percent more than the Navy's estimate.

Submarines

Under the 2015 shipbuilding plan, submarines would overtake surface combatants as the largest source of demand for shipbuilding funds over the next 20 years (see Table 5). The Navy currently operates 14 Ohio class ballistic missile submarines (SSBNs), 4 Ohio class guided missile submarines (SSGNs) modified from the SSBN version, and 55 attack submarines (SSNs) of several classes. Over the next three decades, the Navy plans to buy 12 new SSBNs starting in 2021; 48 new SSNs, including 31 Virginia class submarines (mostly at an average rate of 1.5 per year through 2033); and 17 submarines based on a redesign and improvement of the Virginia class, with production scheduled to begin in

2034. The Navy does not plan to replace its 4 SSGNs when they are retired in the mid- to late 2020s.

Ohio Replacement Ballistic Missile Submarines. SSBNs carry Trident ballistic missiles and are the sea-based leg of the United States' strategic triad for delivering nuclear weapons. (The other two legs are land-based intercontinental ballistic missiles and manned strategic bombers.) The design, cost, and capabilities of the Ohio Replacement submarine class are among the most significant uncertainties in the Navy's and CBO's analyses of the cost of future shipbuilding. Under the 2015 plan, the first Ohio Replacement submarine—sometimes called the SSBN(X)—would be purchased in 2021, although advance procurement funds would be needed starting in 2016 for items with long lead times. The second submarine would be purchased in 2024, followed by 1 per year from 2026 to 2035 (see Figure 3 on page 7). [22]

The Navy currently estimates the cost of the first Ohio Replacement submarine at $12.4 billion in 2014 dollars. The estimated average cost of follow-on ships is now $6.0 billion, which implies a total cost for 12 submarines of $79 billion, or an average of $6.6 billion each. However, the Navy has stated an objective of reducing that $6.0 billion figure to $5.5 billion.[23]

The Navy's estimate represents considerable improvement in the cost per thousand tons of the first Ohio Replacement submarine compared with the first Virginia submarine—an improvement that would affect costs for the entire new class of ballistic missile submarines. The main reason for those improved costs by weight

---

22. For more information, see Ronald O'Rourke, *Navy SSBN(X) Ballistic Missile Submarine Program: Background and Issues for Congress,* Report for Congress R41129 (Congressional Research Service, July 31, 2014); and the testimony of Eric J. Labs, Senior Analyst for Naval Forces and Weapons, Congressional Budget Office, before the Subcommittee on Seapower and Expeditionary Forces of the House Committee on Armed Services, *The Long-Term Outlook for the U.S. Navy's Fleet* (January 20, 2010), www.cbo.gov/publication/41886.

23. Briefing by the Navy to the staff of the House Committee on Armed Services, CBO, and the Congressional Research Service, February 28, 2011. The Navy's numbers in that briefing, expressed in 2010 dollars, were $5.6 billion for the average follow-on submarine, with an objective of reducing that cost to $4.9 billion. Although the Navy's 2015 plan does not yet reflect it, the Navy's Ohio Replacement Program Office currently estimates that it has already reduced the cost to $5.4 billion in 2010 dollars.

Table 5.

Total Shipbuilding Costs, by Major Category, 1985 to 2044

	Historical				CBO's Estimates Under the Navy's 2015 Plan			
	1985- 1994	1995- 2004	2005- 2014	1985- 2014	2015- 2024	2025- 2034	2035- 2044	2015- 2044
	Average Annual Costs (Billions of 2014 dollars)							
New-Ship Construction								
Aircraft carriers	1.5	1.8	1.8	1.7	2.4	2.4	2.7	2.5
Submarines	6.1	2.6	4.1	4.3	7.1	11.2	5.3	7.9
Surface combatants	7.4	4.7	4.2	5.4	5.2	5.2	7.5	6.0
Amphibious ships	1.4	1.5	1.7	1.5	1.1	2.3	1.8	1.8
Logistics and support ships	1.7	0.4	0.8	1.0	0.9	1.4	0.1	0.8
Subtotal	18.2	10.9	12.5	13.9	16.7	22.5	17.5	18.9
Carrier and Submarine Refuelings[a]	0.4	0.9	1.3	0.9	1.4	1.0	0.6	1.0
Other Items	1.1	1.2	0.6	1.0	1.2	0.7	0.6	0.8
Total	**19.6**	**13.0**	**14.5**	**15.7**	**19.2**	**24.2**	**18.7**	**20.7**
	Percentage of Average Annual Costs							
New-Ship Construction								
Aircraft carriers	9	16	14	12	12	10	15	12
Submarines	34	24	32	31	37	46	29	38
Surface combatants	41	43	33	39	27	21	40	29
Amphibious ships	8	14	14	11	6	10	10	8
Logistics and support ships	9	3	6	7	4	6	0	4
Subtotal	92	84	87	88	87	93	94	91
Carrier and Submarine Refuelings[a]	2	7	9	5	7	4	3	5
Other Items	6	9	4	6	6	3	3	4
Total	**100**	**100**	**100**	**100**	**100**	**100**	**100**	**100**

Source: Congressional Budget Office.

Note: Costs of new-ship construction exclude funds for some activities that are typically funded in the Navy's shipbuilding accounts, such as refueling of nuclear-powered aircraft carriers, ship conversions, construction of ships that are not part of the Navy's battle force (oceanographic survey ships, for instance), training ships, outfitting and postdelivery (which include the purchase of many smaller tools and pieces of equipment that are needed to operate a ship but are not necessarily provided by the manufacturing shipyard as part of ship construction), and smaller items. Costs for the mission packages for littoral combat ships, which are not funded in the Navy's shipbuilding accounts, also are not included.

a.   CBO's estimates under the Navy's 2015 plan reflect only the costs of refueling aircraft carriers. Historically, the refueling of nuclear-powered submarines was also included in the Navy's shipbuilding accounts. In 2010, however, the Navy transferred the funding for those refuelings to other accounts.

for the Ohio Replacement is that the Navy will recycle, to the extent possible, the design, technology, and parts used for the Virginia class. Furthermore, because ballistic missile submarines (like the Ohio Replacements) tend to be larger and less dense ships than attack submarines (like the Virginia class), they will be easier to build and therefore less expensive on a weight basis, the Navy argues.

Yet the historical record for the lead ships of new classes of submarines in the 1970s and 1980s provides little reason to believe that ballistic missile submarines are cheaper by weight to build than attack submarines (see Figure 8). The first Ohio class submarine was more expensive to build than the lead ships of the two classes of attack submarines built during the same period—the Los Angeles

Figure 8.

Cost per Thousand Tons of Various Classes of Submarine, Lead Ship and Class Average

Millions of 2014 Dollars

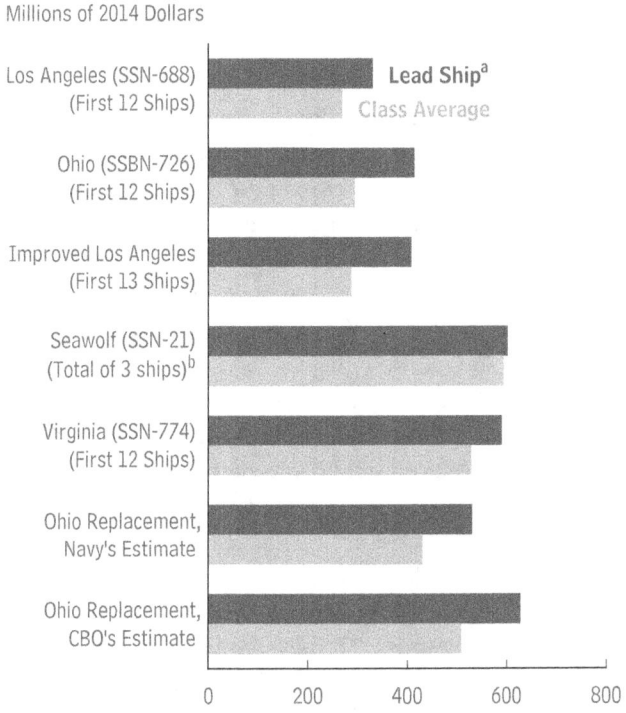

Source: Congressional Budget Office based on data from the Department of the Navy.

Note: Cost per thousand tons of Condition A-1 displacement (the weight of the submarine without its crew, materiel, weapons, or fuel), which is analogous to lightship displacement for surface ships.

a.   Data exclude costs for plans, which comprise nonrecurring engineering and detail design.

b.   Although 29 Seawolf class submarines were planned, only 3 were built.

and the Improved Los Angeles (which made design changes to the Los Angeles that included the addition of 12 vertical launch system cells). In addition, the average costs by weight of the first 12 or 13 ships of the Ohio, Los Angeles, and Improved Los Angeles classes were virtually identical. By the 1990s, the costs of lead ships for submarines had grown substantially, with both the first Seawolf submarine and first Virginia submarine costing about the same by weight—even though the Seawolf is 20 percent larger and was built nine years earlier than the first Virginia.

Using data from the Virginia class submarine program, CBO estimates that the first Ohio Replacement submarine will cost $13.8 billion in 2014 dollars. Estimating

the cost of the first submarine of a class with an entirely new design is particularly difficult because of uncertainty about how much the Navy will spend on nonrecurring engineering and detail design. All told, 12 Ohio Replacement submarines would cost $92 billion in CBO's estimation, or an average of $7.7 billion each—$1.1 billion more per boat than the Navy's estimate. That average includes the $13.8 billion estimated cost of the lead submarine and a $7.1 billion average estimated cost for the 2nd through 12th submarines. Research and development would cost an additional $10 billion to $15 billion, for a total program cost of $102 billion to $107 billion, CBO estimates.

Overall, the Navy expects a 19 percent improvement in the cost-to-weight relationship of the Ohio Replacement class compared with the first 12 of the Virginia class. CBO estimates a 4 percent improvement, which is based in part on savings that will probably be achieved because of projected concurrent production of the Ohio Replacement and Virginia class submarines.

Attack Submarines. Under the 2015 plan, the Navy would buy 31 Virginia class attack submarines. Between 2015 and 2033, those purchases would occur mostly at a rate alternating between 1 and 2 per year. In 2034, the Navy would switch to an improved Virginia class but maintain the same build rate of 1 or 2 per year. With such a procurement schedule, the attack submarine force would remain at or above the Navy's goal of 48 submarines through 2024 but would then fall to between 41 and 47 submarines between 2025 and 2034 before reaching or exceeding 48 submarines again beginning in 2035 (see Figure 4 on page 9).

Senior Navy leaders have stated that Virginia class SSNs would have to cost $2.8 billion or less apiece for the Navy to be able to afford 2 per year.[24] The President's 2015 budget indicates a current cost of those vessels of $2.6 billion each. For the entirety of the Virginia class under the 2015 shipbuilding plan, the Navy's and CBO's estimates are virtually the same: The Navy estimates that the total cost for all 31 of the Virginia class submarines purchased between 2015 and 2044 would be about $88 billion, and CBO estimates that cost at $90 billion.

24.   Specifically, the Navy has said that to purchase 2 Virginia class submarines a year, the cost would have to decline to $2.0 billion each in 2005 dollars, which is equivalent to $2.8 billion in 2014 dollars.

The Navy expects to begin purchasing the improved Virginia class submarine in 2034. The service's recent shipbuilding plans call for the continuing evolution of the current submarine—as a new class of submarine—to incorporate significant technological upgrades in systems and capabilities. CBO similarly assumed that the improved Virginias would incorporate changes that were sufficiently important to make the submarines a new class, although not with a wholly new design. On the basis of that assumption, CBO estimated, the average submarine would cost $3.2 billion, whereas the Navy's estimate was $2.9 billion under the 2015 plan. For reasons that are not clear, the Navy's estimate is a reduction from an average cost of $3.3 billion under the 2014 plan.

Although the Navy's plan does not include submarines to replace the existing SSGNs when they retire in the 2020s, the service expects to lengthen the hull of future Virginia class submarines to insert the Virginia Payload Module (VPM). The VPM would contain four large-diameter payload tubes, each of which could carry seven Tomahawk missiles. That change would increase the submerged displacement of the submarine by nearly 30 percent and would raise the number of the Virginia class's vertical-launch weapons from 12 to 40 (in addition to the 27 weapons in the torpedo room). The Navy estimates that 20 Virginia class submarines equipped with the additional payload modules would provide a "near equivalent" to the strike capability of the existing force of 4 SSGNs. The President's 2015 budget proposed spending $700 million between 2015 and 2019 for research and development on the payload module and for modifying the design of the Virginia class. The Navy's 2015 plan, in contrast to earlier plans, now includes building Virginia class submarines with the VPM beginning in 2021. Both the Navy's and CBO's estimates of costs reflect that change. Neither the Navy nor CBO assumes that the improved Virginia class will include the module.

Large Surface Combatants

The Navy's 2015 plan incorporates the purchase of the same types of destroyers as the 2014 plan. The service restarted production of DDG-51 Flight IIA destroyers in 2010 and purchased 8 ships through 2014 (in addition to the 62 ships that had been purchased when production was initially stopped in 2005). The Navy plans to purchase 3 more DDG-51 Flight IIAs through 2016. Beginning in 2016 and continuing through 2029, the Navy plans to purchase 27 DDG-51s with an upgraded

design, a configuration known as Flight III. In 2030, the Navy would start buying 33 DDG(X)s, a not-yet-designed destroyer intended to replace the DDG-51 class.

The Navy is also pursuing two other strategies to boost its inventory of large surface combatants. One is to modernize 11 of its Ticonderoga class cruisers and thereby extend their service in the fleet through 2043. If the Navy does not modernize those ships, all of the Navy's cruisers would be retired by 2028 (see Box 2 on page 11). The other critical strategy is to keep all DDG-51 Flight IIAs and subsequent destroyers serving in the fleet for 40 years. The class was originally designed to serve for 30 years, but the Navy has gradually increased the planned service life—first to 35 years and then, in the 2009 shipbuilding plan, to 40 years—of Flight IIA and Flight III ships. Of the last 13 classes of destroyers and cruisers, 12 have been retired after serving for 30 years or less. Indeed, in recent years, Spruance class destroyers and some Ticonderoga class cruisers have been retired after serving 25 years or less. The Navy retired those destroyers for various reasons: They reached the end of their useful service lives, they became too expensive to maintain in the waning years of their service lives, or they no longer had the combat capabilities needed to meet existing threats and modernization was not considered cost-effective.[25] If the DDG-51 class met the same fate, then additional ship purchases would be needed to achieve the Navy's inventory goal.

Taken together, the intended ship purchases, cruiser modernization, and extended service lives for destroyers would allow the Navy to meet or exceed its inventory goal of 88 large surface combatants in most years through 2044 (see Figure 4 on page 9).

DDG-51 Flight IIAs. The Navy's existing force of 62 DDG-51 destroyers was built in three primary configurations. The first 28 ships, designated Flight I or II, did not include a hangar for embarking helicopters—which play important roles in countering enemy submarines, attacks by small boats, and, to a lesser degree, mines. The next 34 ships, designated Flight IIA, included a hangar and were therefore able to carry two helicopters or several

---

25. See the testimony of Eric J. Labs, Senior Analyst, Congressional Budget Office, before the Subcommittee on Seapower and Expeditionary Forces of the House Committee on Armed Services, *The Navy's Surface Combatant Programs* (July 31, 2008), www.cbo.gov/publication/20065.

ship-launched unmanned aerial vehicles.[26] In the Navy's 2015 plan, 3 new DDG-51s purchased through 2016 (in addition to 8 purchased between 2010 and 2014 but not yet in the fleet) would use the Flight IIA configuration but would also incorporate the latest ballistic missile defense capabilities.[27] Those ships would have an average cost of $1.4 billion, in CBO's estimation.

DDG-51 Flight IIIs. The Navy's strategy to meet combatant commanders' demands for greater ballistic missile defense capabilities than is provided by existing DDG-51s—and to replace 11 Ticonderoga class cruisers when they are retired in the 2020s—is to modify the design of the DDG-51 Flight IIA destroyer substantially, creating a Flight III configuration.[28] That configuration would incorporate the new Air and Missile Defense Radar (AMDR), now under development, which is larger and more powerful than the radar on earlier DDG-51s. The effective operation of the AMDR in the new Flight III configuration, however, will require increasing the amount of electrical power and cooling available on a Flight III.[29]

With those changes and associated increases in the ship's displacement, a DDG-51 Flight III destroyer would cost about $300 million—or about 20 percent—more than a new Flight IIA destroyer, CBO estimates.[30] Thus, CBO expects that the average cost per ship over the entire production run would be $1.9 billion, or about 19 percent more than the Navy's estimate of $1.6 billion.

CBO's estimate of the costs of the DDG Flight IIA and Flight III ships to be purchased in the future is a little less than it was last year. Most of the decrease for the Flight III can be attributed to updated information on the cost of incorporating the AMDR into the Flight III configuration. The cost of the AMDR itself, according to the Navy, has declined steadily through the development program, and DoD's Cost Analysis and Program Evaluation (CAPE) office concurs with the reduced estimate. The Navy decreased its estimate for the average price of a DDG-51 Flight III ship from $1.8 billion in the 2014 plan to $1.6 billion in the 2015 plan, primarily as a result of continued reductions in the estimate of the cost of the AMDR. Considerable uncertainty remains in the DDG-51 Flight III program, however. Costs could be higher or lower than CBO's estimate, depending on the eventual cost and complexity of the AMDR, along with associated changes in the ship's design to integrate the new radar.

DDG(X) Future Guided Missile Destroyers. Like the Navy's 2014 shipbuilding plan, the current plan includes a future class of destroyers intended to replace the DDG-51 Flight I and II ships when they retire in the late 2020s and 2030s.[31] The Navy's 2015 plan describes the ship as a "mid-sized future surface combatant" but does not provide further specification.[32] CBO has adopted a generic DDG(X) designation, implying an unknown design.

---

26. For a detailed discussion of the differences between the DDG-51 flights, see Norman Polmar, *The Naval Institute Guide to the Ships and Aircraft of the U.S. Fleet,* 19th ed. (Naval Institute Press, 2013), pp. 140–145.

27. The Navy has announced that all existing DDG-51s will eventually be equipped with improved ballistic missile defenses; up to 33 of those upgrades were funded by the end of fiscal year 2014. For more about the Navy's plans for the DDG-51 program, see Ronald O'Rourke, *Navy DDG-51 and DDG-1000 Destroyer Programs: Background and Issues for Congress,* Report for Congress RL32109 (Congressional Research Service, July 31, 2014).

28. Combatant commanders—the four-star generals or admirals who head the regional commands—are responsible for all U.S. military operations within their geographic areas.

29. See Ronald O'Rourke, *Navy Aegis Ballistic Missile Defense (BMD) Program: Background and Issues for Congress,* Report for Congress RL33745 (Congressional Research Service, November 7, 2014), and *Navy DDG-51 and DDG-1000 Destroyer Programs: Background and Issues for Congress,* Report for Congress RL32109 (Congressional Research Service, July 31, 2014). Press reports indicate that some Navy officials do not agree with the DDG-51 Flight III strategy and would prefer to build Flight IIAs a little longer while designing an entirely new destroyer that would allow for greater growth potential in all respects. See Christopher P. Cavas, "U.S. Navy Weighs Halving LCS Order," *Defense News* (March 17, 2013), http://tinyurl.com/kbey7qp.

30. As a point of comparison, the Navy's first Flight IIA ship—the DDG-79, which incorporated such changes as a helicopter hangar and a larger displacement—cost about 20 percent more than the DDG-78. The transition from the Flight IIA to Flight III ships is expected to involve more extensive changes than the transition from the Flight I/II to Flight IIA ships.

31. That retirement date is based on the Navy's assumption that all DDG-51 Flight IIAs will be modernized midway through their service life and will operate for 40 years.

32. Department of the Navy, *Report to Congress on the Annual Long-Range Plan for Construction of Naval Vessels for FY 2015* (June 2014), p. 15, http://go.usa.gov/FYZR (PDF, 3.4 MB). This description did not appear in previous shipbuilding plans.

Under the 2015 plan, production of the DDG(X) would start in 2030, which would make it a successor to the DDG-51 Flight III program. The Navy says that it would buy 35 DDG(X)s at an average cost of $1.8 billion, or about $200 million more than the cost of DDG-51 Flight III ships. Those cost estimates imply that the DDG(X)'s capabilities would represent a relatively modest improvement over those of the DDG-51 Flight III or (if capabilities were significantly improved) the DDG(X) would be a smaller ship than the DDG-51 Flight III.

CBO expects that the DDG(X) will have a largely new design but will be about the same size as the DDG-51 Flight III—consistent with the concept of a midsized surface combatant. CBO projects the average cost of the DDG(X) at $2.5 billion, roughly 40 percent higher than the Navy's projection. Over the 2015–2044 period, CBO estimates, the Navy would have to spend $88 billion for the DDG(X) portion of the shipbuilding program—$25 billion more than the Navy's estimate of $63 billion. That difference represents nearly 40 percent of the overall difference of $66 billion between the Navy's and CBO's estimates of the cost of the 2015 shipbuilding plan as a whole.

CBO's current estimate of a $2.5 billion average cost for the DDG(X) is substantially lower than its estimate of $3.4 billion last year. The downward revision reflects CBO's assumption that the DDG(X) would be similar in size to the DDG-51 Flight III, rather than significantly larger as CBO assumed in its estimate of the 2014 plan. The large amount of uncertainty about the ultimate size and capabilities of the DDG(X) suggests that the true cost could be substantially different from either the Navy's or CBO's estimate.

Littoral Combat Ships

In the 2015 plan, the Navy envisions building a force of 52 small surface combatants called littoral combat ships by 2025. The first LCS was authorized in 2005, and the Navy already has 20 of those ships either in its fleet or under construction—10 each of two different designs being built by two different contractors. Because those ships are assumed to have a service life of 25 years, the Navy would need to begin procuring their replacements in 2030. Therefore, the Navy plans to purchase 32 more LCSs through 2025 to complete its initial force of 52 ships and then to purchase 34 next-generation ships, called LCS(X)s, between 2030 and 2044 to replace the first-generation LCSs as they retire.

The LCS differs from past and present U.S. warships in that its production program is divided into two components—the sea frame (the ship itself) and mission packages (the main combat systems). The sea frame is being designed and built so that mission packages can be switched on a given ship over time as the ship's mission changes. Currently, the Navy expects to use three types of mission packages—one each for countering mines, submarines, and surface ships. It also expects that the LCS will be able to perform maritime security operations (such as sanctions enforcement, counterpiracy operations, and engagement with friendly navies) while equipped with any of those mission packages. In all, the service plans to buy 64 mission packages for the 52 ships by 2025.[33] In time, the Navy may also develop and purchase other types of mission packages.[34]

Of the 32 additional LCSs that the Navy intends to purchase, 4 are planned to be purchased in 2015 and 2016—completing the 10-ship purchase agreements with the two existing shipbuilders—and an additional 8 in 2016 through 2018, under contractual arrangements that have not yet been announced.[35] Therefore, the Navy expects to have 32 LCSs in the fleet or under construction by the end of 2018 and plans to purchase 20 more between 2019 and 2025.

However, the Navy's plans for the LCS were called into question earlier this year by the Secretary of Defense. On February 24, 2014, the Secretary expressed concerns that the LCS and its associated mission packages, as currently designed, were not survivable enough and lacked offensive firepower to operate independently and effectively against potential future adversaries that employ the most advanced antiship technologies and weapon systems.[36] He ordered the Navy not to contract for more than

33. Department of the Navy, *Report to Congress: Littoral Combat Ship Mission Packages* (May 2009).

34. For more detail on the LCS program, see Ronald O'Rourke, *Navy Littoral Combat Ship (LCS) Program: Background and Issues for Congress*, Report for Congress RL33741 (Congressional Research Service, August 4, 2014).

35. Although the Navy already has 20 LCSs in its fleet or under construction, 4 of those ships were purchased between 2005 and 2009 prior to the two 10-ship contracts. Thus, the Navy needs to purchase 4 more ships to complete those contracts.

36. Secretary of Defense Chuck Hagel, memorandum to the Secretary of the Navy and Chief of Naval Operations on the Littoral Combat Ship Program (February 24, 2014).

32 ships until it studied those issues and made proposals to "procure a capable and lethal small surface combatant, generally consistent with the capabilities of a frigate" by considering "a completely new design, existing ship designs (including the LCS), and a modified LCS." The proposals were to be submitted in sufficient time to inform the President's 2016 budget submission.

On December 11, 2014, the Secretary of the Defense announced the results of that study: He has decided that the last 20 ships will be modified from the two existing LCS designs to include additional offensive weapons and survivability features. Those changes would begin with the ships planned for purchase in 2019. The Navy's 2015 shipbuilding program does not incorporate any additional costs that may be incurred as a result of the recent decision. In its December 2014 announcement, DoD estimated that its proposed changes would increase the cost of an LCS by a little less than 20 percent.

In the 2015 Future Years Defense Program, the Navy estimates the average cost of the LCS at about $420 million per ship over the next five years, including the 10 ships to be purchased from 2016 through 2019, after the end of the two 10-ship contracts. That figure is well below the Congressionally mandated cost cap for the LCS program of $515 million per ship (adjusted for inflation).[37] Overall, the Navy estimates that the 32 LCSs to be purchased by 2025—designated by the Navy as Flight 0—would cost about $464 million per ship, on average, which does not include any additional costs to make the LCS more capable of surviving attacks or more lethal to adversaries.

Since its analysis of the Navy's 2012 shipbuilding plan, CBO has lowered its estimate for the cost of the LCSs purchased between 2010 and 2015 to reflect the prices and terms to which the Navy and the two shipyards agreed. However, CBO expects that the Navy will pay slightly higher prices for the ships purchased after 2015, in part because the annual procurement quantities planned for those years are lower than in previous years.

In addition, CBO anticipated that changes in the design of the LCS in response to the Secretary's directive would add 15 percent to the cost of the last 20 LCSs, which CBO calls the Flight 1 ships but the Navy calls small surface combatants. Based on that assumption, CBO expects that those ships would cost an average of $600 million each. (CBO completed its analysis before the Secretary of Defense announced his decision about the configuration of those last ships, which DoD anticipates will add a little less than 20 percent to their cost. CBO will reexamine that issue in its analysis of the 2016 shipbuilding plan.)

Under the 2015 plan, the Navy would also buy 34 next-generation littoral combat ships—called LCS(X)s—beginning in 2030. Both the Navy and CBO assumed that the LCS(X)s would have the capabilities of the Flight 0 ships they would be replacing rather than those of the later Flight 1 ships. The Navy's cost estimate for an LCS(X) is $473 million, just slightly more (after adjusting for inflation) than the expected average cost of an LCS Flight 0. CBO estimates the average cost of the LCS(X) would be a little higher, about $500 million per ship. CBO's current estimate is less than its estimate last year, when CBO assumed that the LCS(X) would look more like the proposed Flight 1. If the LCX(X) were designed to meet or exceed the capabilities of the LCS Flight 1, then its cost would probably be higher than the Navy and CBO now estimate.

Amphibious Warfare Ships

The Navy's inventory goal for amphibious warfare ships is 33. The proposed force would consist of 11 LHA or LHD amphibious assault ships, 11 LPD amphibious transport docks, and 11 replacements for the Navy's LSD dock landing ships. In pursuit of that force, the 2015 plan calls for buying 7 LHA-6s, at a rate of 1 every four or seven years, to replace LHD-1 class amphibious assault ships as they are retired.[38] The plan envisions buying 11 LX(R)s (the replacement for LSDs), 1 every other year between 2020 and 2028 and then 1 per year until 2034, to replace existing dock landing ships in the LSD-41 and LSD-49 classes. Under the 2015 plan, the LX(R) would enter the fleet one year later than under the 2014 plan. (This is the third consecutive shipbuilding plan in which the Navy has delayed the start of the LSD replacement class by one year.) The 2015 plan would also start

---

37. The National Defense Authorization Act for Fiscal Year 2010, which set the LCS cost cap that would apply to ships purchased in fiscal year 2010 and beyond, gave the Secretary of the Navy authority to waive compliance with the cap if doing so was considered in "the best interest of the United States," if the ship was "affordable, within the context of the annual naval vessel construction plan," or in other specific circumstances.

38. There is a seven-year gap between the ship purchased in 2017 and the next one purchased in 2024. After that, however, the LHA class is purchased at a rate of 1 every four years.

replacing the LPD-17 class with a new class in the early 2040s, buying 1 ship each in 2040, 2042, and 2044.

The Navy also intends to keep the existing class of LHD-1 amphibious assault ships in service for 43 to 45 years. That expectation, which was also stated in the 2013 and 2014 plans, represents an increase relative to the 40-year service life incorporated in the 2012 plan.

With that procurement schedule and those intended service lives, the total number of amphibious warfare ships would be at or above the goal of 33 ships for about two-thirds of the 30-year period covered by the plan (see Figure 4 on page 9). After 2015, the number of such ships would never fall short of the goal by more than 2 ships.

The Navy estimates that the LHA-6 class amphibious assault ships will cost $3.7 billion apiece. CBO's estimate for those ships is slightly higher: an average of $4.0 billion per ship. Both CBO and the Navy assumed that the LHA-6 class ship authorized for 2016 and all subsequent amphibious assault ships would include well decks, necessitating some redesign of the LHA-6 class—and therefore additional costs. (Well decks are large floodable areas in the sterns of most amphibious warfare ships that allow amphibious vehicles and craft to be launched directly from the ships.) Those costs are included in both the Navy's and CBO's estimates.

For the LX(R), the Navy estimates an average cost of $1.4 billion per ship. Since the publication of the Navy's 2015 plan, press reports have indicated that the service wants the LX(R) to be based on the hull of the LPD-17, which is much larger than existing LSDs. An LPD-17 ordered today would cost about $2.1 billion. Therefore, to meet its estimate for the cost of the LX(R), the Navy would need to make significant changes to the ships and the manner in which it buys them. First, the LX(R) variant of the LPD-17 would need to have substantially less

capability than the LPD-17 class. The Navy has not yet released any specifications or details about the capabilities it intends to include in the LX(R). Second, the Navy would need to adopt a competitive process for procurement and probably also ask the Congress to give it multiyear, or "block buy," authority to purchase ships—or at least their materials—in batches of 5 to 10. Such authority would be similar to the multiyear contracts the Navy employs for the Arleigh Burke class destroyers and to the block buy contracts the Navy uses for Virginia class attack submarines and littoral combat ships. If the Navy did open the LX(R) to competition, the shipyards bidding for the right to build the ships would probably incorporate the benefits of those types of contracts into their bids.

Based on the limited information available now, CBO estimates the cost of the LX(R) at an average of $1.8 billion per ship. CBO used the existing LPD-17 hull as the starting point for its estimate and then adjusted the ship's size to reflect the reduced capability it expects for the LX(R). CBO's estimate also accounts for the use of multiyear or block buy procurement authority in a potentially competitive environment. Various factors could cause the actual cost to be above or below the estimate. For example, it is not clear that the Navy would be able to conduct a full and open competition for the LX(R) in light of the fact that the yard currently building the LPD-17 class, Ingalls of Huntington-Ingalls Industries, would presumably enter the bidding with a significant advantage. The Navy might also have a limited ability to benefit from competition for the LX(R) if the Congress directed the Navy to ensure that all of the shipyards building the Navy's ships received enough business to remain profitable. In contrast, if the Navy designs and builds the LX(R) in ways that are substantially different from the methods used for the LPD-17, then the cost of the new ships could be less than CBO estimates.

Appendix:
Comparison of CBO's and the Navy's Cost Estimates for Individual Ship Programs

Each year the Navy provides estimates of the costs of building each class of ship in its 30-year shipbuilding plan. The Congressional Budget Office also produces annual estimates. Table A-1 presents a comparison of the two sets of figures for the past four 30-year plans.

Table A-1.

Difference Between CBO's and the Navy's Cost Estimates for Individual Ship Programs

Percentage of Total Cost Difference

Ship Program	2012 Plan	2013 Plan	2014 Plan	2015 Plan
CVN-78 Gerald R. Ford Class Aircraft Carriers	18	13	3	3
Ohio Replacement Ballistic Missile Submarines	15	13	12	20
Virginia Class Attack Submarines	1	1	-1	3
Improved Virginia Class Attack Submarines (Replacements for Virginia class)	3	4	-3	8
DDG-51 Arleigh Burke Class Destroyers				
Flight IIA	3	0	0	0
Flight III	-7	11	7	11
DDG(X) Destroyers (Replacements for Arleigh Burke class)	41	34	58	38
Littoral Combat Ships	1	3	4	5
LCS(X)s (Replacements for littoral combat ships)	5	4	7	0
LX(R)s (Replacements for amphibious dock landing ships)	5	4	4	5
LHA-6 Amphibious Assault Ships	7	5	5	3
T-AO(X) Oilers	0	0	1	1
Other	8	7	4	4
Total	**100**	**100**	**100**	**100**
Memorandum:				
Difference in Billions of Dollars[a]	74	94	76	66

Source: Congressional Budget Office.

Note: Numbers reflect the percentage of the total cost difference between CBO's and the Navy's estimates for each plan: Positive values indicate instances in which CBO's estimate is higher; negative values, instances in which the Navy's is higher.

a. For each plan, the difference is expressed in constant dollars from the preceding year. For instance, the value for the 2012 plan is expressed in 2011 dollars; for the 2013 plan, in 2012 dollars; and so on.

List of Tables and Figures

Tables

Figures

About This Document

This Congressional Budget Office report was prepared as required by the National Defense Authorization Act for Fiscal Year 2012 (Public Law 112-81). In accordance with CBO's mandate to provide objective, impartial analysis, the report makes no recommendations.

Eric J. Labs of CBO's National Security Division prepared the report with guidance from David Mosher and Matthew Goldberg. Raymond Hall of CBO's Budget Analysis Division produced the cost estimates with guidance from Sarah Jennings. Daniel Frisk of CBO provided helpful comments on the report, as did Brian McGrath of the Hudson Institute's Center for American Seapower and Russell Rumbaugh of the Stimson Center. (The existence of external reviewers implies no responsibility for the final product, which rests solely with CBO.)

Jeffrey Kling, John Skeen, and Robert Sunshine reviewed this report, Juyne Linger edited it, and Maureen Costantino prepared it for publication. An electronic version is available on CBO's website (www.cbo.gov/publication/49818).

Douglas W. Elmendorf
Director

December 2014